BIG WALL CLIMBING:
Elite Technique

MOUNTAINEERS
OUTDOOR EXPERT
series

BIG WALL CLIMBING:
Elite Technique

Jared Ogden

THE MOUNTAINEERS BOOKS

DEDICATION

To my wife, Kristin, and son, Tobin,
who have given me great inspiration, patience, and understanding.

THE MOUNTAINEERS BOOKS
is the nonprofit publishing arm of The Mountaineers Club,
an organization founded in 1906 and dedicated to the exploration,
preservation, and enjoyment of outdoor and wilderness areas.

1001 SW Klickitat Way, Suite 201, Seattle, WA 98134

© 2005 by Jared Ogden

First edition, 2005

Published simultaneously in Great Britain by Cordee, 3a DeMontfort Street, Leicester, England, LE1 7HD

Manufactured in China

Acquiring Project Editor: Mary Metz
Copy Editor: Kris Fulsaas
Cover and Book Design: The Mountaineers Books
Layout: Marge Mueller, Gray Mouse Graphics
Illustrator: Jeremy Collins; Illustration on page 110 from *Mountaineering: The Freedom of the Hills,*
    7th edition, The Mountaineers Books
All photographs by the author unless otherwise noted.

Cover photograph: *Author free climbing pitch 12, (5.13 R), Hallucinogen Wall, Black Canyon of the*
    Gunnison National Park © Topher Donahue
Frontispiece: *Willy Benegas on Electric Ladyland (V 5.11 A3), Yosemite National Park*
Backcover photograph: *Mark Synnott on Parallel Worlds, Great Trango Tower*

Library of Congress Cataloging-in-Publication Data
Ogden, Jared, 1971-
  Big walls : elite technique / Jared Ogden.— 1st ed.
    p. cm.
  Includes bibliographical references.
  ISBN 0-89886-748-7
  1. Rock climbing—Training. I. Title.
  GV200.2.O43 2005
  796.52'23—dc22

                                   2005000334

 Printed on recycled paper

Contents

CHAPTER 1

Wall-Climbing Fundamentals

CHAPTER 2

Basic Wall-Climbing Procedures

Acknowledgments

This book is the culmination of years spent learning the skills necessary to scale big walls, and I owe a tremendous amount of thanks and appreciation to all my climbing partners who shared these experiences while living in the vertical world. I might never have braved to venture into climbing had it not been for all the inspirational climbers whose vision and enthusiasm came before me, and I want this book to continue inspiring many more climbers into the future.

Thanks to Mike Gibbs for his help with the hauling systems. Thanks also to Mary Metz and the entire staff at The Mountaineers Books for being persistent in getting this book published and to Kris Fulsaas for her excellent job editing the manuscript.

Introduction

Big wall climbing is the process of scaling a cliff that's 1500 feet tall or bigger that requires from one to several days to climb using multipitch leading techniques, possibly using portaledges and hauling equipment. Big wall climbing differs from other forms of climbing simply due to the duration of the climb; the verticality and steepness, minimum amount of large features such as chimneys and ledges, and size of the cliff; the need to haul equipment; and the use of portaledges rather than natural features for bivies. The best-known big wall in the world is El Capitan in California's Yosemite National Park: its massive, 3000-foot overhanging vertical face with few ledges and small cracks clearly defines a big wall.

Big wall routes tend to follow incipient cracks and features that are too small to free climb, which means aid climbing is required, although free and aid climbing are often used in unison to piece together a route. Aid, or artificial, climbing means you use etriers (aiders), pitons, hooks, and other aid climbing–specific equipment to support your weight as you make upward progress; free climbing means you use your hands and feet on the rock to make upward progress without weighting protection, which you use only to protect yourself from taking a long fall.

Clean aid climbing, also known as "French-free," means you use etriers to support your weight, and protection that doesn't require hammering to place—such as camming devices, stoppers, hexes, and slider nuts—to make upward progress. Clean aid climbing—aid climbing without a hammer and pitons—is used on a lot of "trade" routes (those that have had a lot of travel) in places such as Canyonlands,

Yosemite, and Zion National Parks. Clean aid has gained momentum with advances in gear technology and in the hope that clean aid climbing will save the rock from excessive damage and scarring. Clean aid climbing is a great way to learn the process of aid climbing; for your first few walls, it is a good way to go before you step up and get on something that's more difficult.

The traditional big wall involves predominantly aid climbing, which is slow and tedious, forcing climbers to spend several days on the wall in order to complete the climb. However, today there are plenty of walls that can be climbed in a day or less, depending on how fast and skilled a climber you are.

For instance, a proficient free climber who has multipitch experience and some knowledge of clean aid or French-free climbing could climb the South Face route (1500 feet; V, 5.10a, A2) on Washington Column in Yosemite in a day, whereas a novice climber without this experience would probably need at least two days. In the Black Canyon of the Gunnison National Monument in Colorado, the majority of routes on the 1500- to 2700-foot walls are climbs that are usually done in a day, either all-free or with a little A0, and climbers can scale one of these big walls without hauling bivy gear or spending days on the climb.

Climbing a big wall such as El Capitan will indelibly change your life, and the experience will be forever ingrained in your memory. On my first climb of a big wall, I had no idea what I needed other than bravery. My knees knocked, my palms sweated, and my mind raced at the thought of dangling off a 3000-foot cliff. I toughed it out and had the time of my life hanging out up there for days on end. Now I look back nostalgically at my inexperience and at how everything I went through climbing that first wall changed my life forever. I challenged my endurance, tested my bravery, learned new skills, and, most important, got hooked on big walls.

HOW TO USE THIS BOOK

Back when I made my first big wall climb, there were no instructional books on wall climbing or even rock climbing gyms in which to practice. I learned wall climbing by climbing walls. When I began to write this book, it seemed as monumental a challenge as completing a grade VII wall climb. In the process of writing it, I've learned many new tricks while rethinking old standards to provide the best possible resource for your big wall climbing adventures.

Whether you're a weekend warrior or a full-on wall addict, this step-by-step instructional book has everything you need to get up a big wall. In Chapter 1, Wall-Climbing Fundamentals, you'll learn the tools of the trade and how to use them, ratings, how to choose your partners and routes, and big wall style and ethics. Chapter 2, Basic Wall-Climbing Procedures, focuses on different leading and hauling scenarios and why some are better suited than others, staying on route, multiple following setups for different terrain, belaying, and how to retreat if necessary. Chapter 3, Advanced Techniques, covers speed climbing tactics, how to live on a wall for several days or a week or even longer,

the steps involved in doing first ascents, solo climbing, and many other tricks. Chapter 4 focuses on self-rescue techniques. At the back of the book, you'll find a glossary, resources (Appendix A), and an overview of some of the big walls of the world (Appendix B) as well as a suggested reading list.

The methods described in this book aren't necessarily the only way to perform these tasks; it's more an overview of the preferred methods that have been developed over the years and by no means represents every possible way to climb a wall—that would be a nearly impossible task. Each climber will adapt certain methods he or she feels comfortable with and may improvise or create personal methods as he or she sees fit. What you'll find in this book represents what most wall climbers do, and these techniques have been time tested on some of the biggest walls in the world.

This book covers everything you need to get ready for any wall adventure, whether you're undertaking your maiden voyage, you just need to polish up your skills, or you want to learn how to manage your ropes more efficiently. By reading this book, you'll attain a better understanding on the multitude of systems, equipment, commitment, and challenges of wall-climbing. With this book, you'll be able to learn quickly the standard wall-climbing systems and practices necessary to scale any wall, while gaining insight to the modern speed- and free-climbing tactics that have revolutionized wall climbing today.

Most readers may want to learn a bit

more about aid climbing and the systems involved with climbing a big wall; others might want to learn how to be more efficient at it. Either way, this comprehensive guide's illustrations and instruction will have you racked and ready for any big wall adventure. The climbing is up to you.

WHO THIS BOOK IS FOR

This book assumes that the reader is an experienced climber who understands basic climbing terminology and basic climbing practices for multipitch climbing but is in search of more in-depth knowledge on the subject. Climbers attempting a big wall need solid climbing fundamentals, with two years of climbing experience. In addition, it's a good idea (but not mandatory) to have two years of free-climbing experience, including several multipitch climbs and a dozen or so practice aid pitches. The list below represents the basic skills a climber needs to have before learning the more advanced techniques given in this book:

- Basic commands for belaying and rappelling
- Basic techniques for belaying and rappelling
- Knot-tying skills, including figure eight, figure eight follow-through (also called rewoven figure eight), double fishermans, bowline, water knot, overhand, and girth hitch
- Placement skills for traditional clean protection, including stoppers and camming devices

- Setup of a basic two- to three-piece equalized anchor
- Basic multipitch climbing skills, including leading and following

In addition, the big wall climber should be in top physical condition and be able to handle multiple pitches of physical climbing and hard work for several days on end. Doing a few hundred pull-ups a day and hiking for several miles over rugged terrain with a heavy pack are roughly equivalent to climbing a few pitches a day on a big wall.

A SHORT HISTORY OF BIG WALL CLIMBING

It's hard to say definitively where and when the first big wall was climbed. In the early 20th century, climbers were scaling big rock faces in the Dolomites and the European Alps employing free- and aid-climbing tactics to create bold ascents. These climbs presented the crucial mental and physical breakthroughs necessary to spur on future climbers to take on big walls, but for decades the sheer, blank walls sat dormant, waiting to be climbed by future generations with better tools and methods.

In the 1940s, big walls were still considered unclimbable due to their impenetrable faces and sheer magnitude; climbers also faced a lack of sophisticated equipment. Though big walls were beyond the scope of climbing practices and equipment at the time, climbers were starting to see the potential of such climbs, and numerous attempts were made. When John Salathe arrived in Yosemite in the late '40s, his ascents of the Lost Arrow Chimney in 1947 and Sentinel Rock in 1950 ushered in a new style that tackled the big walls through aid climbing.

Then the late 1950s saw the birth of modern big wall climbing in Yosemite with the pioneering first ascents of the northwest face of Half Dome in 1957 and the southeast face of El Capitan in 1958. These walls truly defined big wall climbing: sheer rock faces reaching upward uninterrupted, sporting large roofs with faint cracks and tiny features. Big wall climbing had finally arrived.

Soon after, with the invention and proliferation of hard iron pitons, jumars, and hammocks, wall climbing exploded in the 1960s and 1970s. During this golden age of wall climbing, the limits of aid climbing skyrocketed as technology, attitudes, and style advanced. The wall-climbing techniques and skills developed in Yosemite were then taken to places such as Baffin Island, Pakistan, Patagonia, and beyond to some of the wildest walls on the planet.

The climbing practices for big wall climbing have changed radically in the past few decades, with speed and free climbing taking a firm grip on today's ascents, along with cutting-edge aid climbing and link-ups of several walls in a day. The traditional idea of wall climbing has changed now that routes that used to take days can be climbed by fit speed climbers in under 24 hours. Of course, this isn't for every climber looking for a big wall experience, but it shows the variety of approaches that can be taken. Today, we owe thanks to those courageous individuals who cast out and dared to scale those big walls, showing us the way to the future of big wall climbing.

A NOTE ABOUT SAFETY

Safety is an important concern in all outdoor activities. No book can alert you to every hazard or anticipate the limitations of every reader. The descriptions of techniques and procedures in this book are intended to provide general information. This is not a complete text on climbing technique. Nothing substitutes for formal instruction, routine practice, and plenty of experience. When you follow any of the procedures described here, you assume responsibility for your own safety. Use this book as a general guide to further information.

— *The Mountaineers Books*

CHAPTER 1

Russel Mitchrovitch on The Jet Stream (VI 5.11 A4), Half Dome, Yosemite National Park

Wall-Climbing Fundamentals

In this chapter you'll learn the tools of the trade and what they're used for, how to read and understand climb ratings, the basic movements of aid climbing, proper planning for your objective, and the climbing styles and ethics associated with wall climbing.

GEAR

Wall climbing is gear intensive. It requires more time and equipment than any other discipline of climbing. The tools you'll need to scale a big wall range from the obvious basics of your harness and helmet to accessories such as gloves, kneepads, and a headlamp. When I first got started in wall climbing, I didn't have a lot of the gear, so I improvised and made some of it, and what gear I did have I made do with. Today, there's so much equipment available to

make wall climbing more efficient and safe, while removing the slow and cumbersome ways of the past, that it can be hard to choose what you need. Following are some tips on how to choose what you'll need and what to look for in a quality item that will perform and last over the course of several wall climbs.

HARNESSES

A lot has changed since climbers were using a 2-inch strand of webbing tied in an overhand follow-through knot around their waist for a harness with no leg loops. Back then, a fall was unpleasant and avoided if possible. Today you can find wall-specific harnesses designed with comfort, function, and durability in mind to make the wall-climbing experience more enjoyable than in the past.

When you're going to buy a harness, you must decide whether you need a wall-specific harness, a sport-climbing harness, or a standard free-climbing all-purpose harness. If you're going to do a lot of big walls, consider getting a comfortable wall-specific harness. Alternatively, if you don't want to spend the extra money or think you might not do too many walls, an all-purpose harness will suffice. Using a sport-climbing harness is not a good idea because they tend to make your feet numb after you've hung at a belay for hours on end, and they lack the padding needed for support, as well as other features you need on a big wall. A harness built with heavy-gauge webbing around a well-padded waist belt that has stiff plastic gear loops works best. Some of the key features you'll want built into your harness include the following:

- A minimum of four gear loops on the waist belt, with two on each side that are visible while climbing
- A full-strength rear clip-in point for trailing a tag line or carrying jumars, a pulley, a water bottle, or whatever you might need to keep conveniently close at hand but out of your way
- Detachable drop-seat-style leg loops for going to the bathroom
- A sturdy belay loop

Other features that make for a more comfortable ride include a wider, reinforced waist belt; extra gear loops; adjustable wide leg loops; and a reinforced tie-in point that will stand up to the high friction caused by a lot of wall climbing.

Some harnesses come with full-strength gear loops for added safety. The gear loops should be made with stiff plastic to distribute the weight of the carabiners and gear evenly while you clip and unclip the biners from it.

To simulate what it will be like on the wall, try on your harness loaded up with most of your rack and your tag line clipped

Big wall–specific harness

in to the back to supply enough weight. If the waist belt rolls over or sags off your hips, you need a better fit and a stiffer harness.

Fit. Because you'll be spending a lot of time hanging in your harness at belays and while leading, it's important to get a comfortable one that fits properly. Fit and sizing are very important in your harness. An improper fit will be dangerous and uncomfortable, and you'll want to burn such a harness after your first wall. The three key components to a proper fit are the waist belt, leg loops, and rise.

1. **Waist belt:** Choose one that is about the size of your pant waist size, and be sure that there's enough room to make it tighter or larger without it running out of adjustment. If it's too big you'll never get it tight enough, and if it's too small you won't be able to safely double back the webbing through the buckle, especially if you plan on wearing multiple layers of clothing. If you're having a hard time using the buckle, consider a different harness because you use the buckles on the waist belt and leg loops a lot, and struggling every time you need to get into your harness is a bummer. It is especially difficult when your hands are cold.

2. **Leg loops:** These should either be of a fixed size with a small strip of

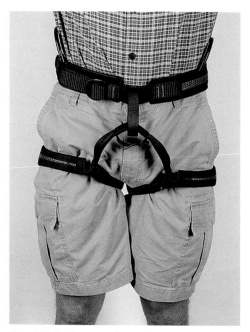

Good-fitting harness, front view

Good-fitting harness, back view

Good-fitting harness, side view

elastic near the risers for an adjustable stretch fit or be adjustable with a buckle allowing you to custom fit them for putting on or taking off clothing while still wearing the waist belt and being tied in. Make sure the loops aren't too small or too big, because if they're too small they will constrict blood flow and be uncomfortable, and if they're too large they won't hold you properly when hanging and can restrict your movement. Find a combination of leg loops and waist belt that fit *you* well because all bodies are different and not all harness sizes fit perfectly in both waist and leg areas.

3. **Rise:** A harness's rise is the distance between the leg loops and the waist belt. It's important to get a harness with the correct rise because this is what distributes your weight evenly while you're hanging in it. If the rise is too long you will tend to fall backward, and if the rise is too short all the weight is on your waist belt. When you are hanging in your harness, you should hang upright. Try this at the gym or shop before you buy a harness to make sure you get one that fits properly.

The comfort of a harness comes from the waist belt and leg loops. Stay clear of unpadded leg loops and waist belts, and look for seams that might chafe, especially on the inside of the groin area. Some wall harnesses are 4–6 inches wide, but be sure the leg loops and waist belt taper toward the front for optimal movement without compromising comfort and support where you need it.

Chest harness. The partner to your main harness is a chest harness. Although not mandatory gear, a chest harness is very useful on a wall. Uses of a chest harness other than to rack your gear include:

- To get a comfortable rest while hanging at a belay, use a sling clipped in to the

Simple, lightweight chest harness

front of the chest harness and clip it to the belay above you, then lean into it in conjunction with your sit harness.

- Use it as a second tie-in point for added security.
- Use it while jumarring a free-hanging fixed rope by clipping in to the top jumar at a height that supports your upper body.
- Use it as a rack while cleaning pitches and keeping your gear organized at belays.

The best kind of chest harness has at least one gear loop on each side, although most have two, with ample padding on the shoulders to support the weight of a wall rack. It should also have a sternum strap to keep it in place. Some chest harnesses come with a full-strength sternum buckle that gives you the option of using it as a second tie-in point, a handy option for solo belay techniques (see Chapter 3, Advanced Techniques). There are chest harnesses on the market that have incorporated hydration systems, stash pockets, and adjustable gear sling lengths for versatility and function. Choose one that will suit your preferences and body type.

HELMET

A helmet is a must when you're climbing big walls. Rockfall, equipment failing and hitting you in the head, dropped items from another party, and leader falls can all contribute to head injuries. Helmets absorb the impact of falling objects and impacts created by a fall by distributing and absorbing the forces across the surface of the helmet and by transferring them safely to your head though the helmet's suspension system.

Most helmets are certified by the Union Internationale des Associations d'Alpinisme (UIAA) for quality assurance and safety control standards. There are so many helmets on the market now that you have a lot of choices. Hard shells consist mostly of plastics, but there are also helmets made of fiberglass, Kevlar-carbon blends, and Styrofoam. Hard-shell helmets have a system of straps that are easily adjusted for different-size heads and are usually well ventilated; Styrofoam helmets are usually very light but lack significant adjustment for multiple users or for the added bulk of a hat worn underneath it. If your Styrofoam helmet does take a solid blow, you should buy a new one. They are designed to absorb the blow once. After a major hit, replace it.

Whatever you choose, make sure it fits well, has ample ventilation, and will hold up under typical use. Be sure you get one that has an adjustable fit system so you can customize the fit for when you're wearing a hat. Proper fit involves making sure that the size of the suspension fits your head (there are multiple sizes), that the helmet doesn't flop around on your head when you move around, and that there is enough room for adjustment in the chin strap. Be sure the helmet covers your forehead and that the back of your helmet doesn't ride on the back of your head with the chin strap choking you.

Get one that is light in color, to reflect heat and to be visible from afar. Other

Three helmets suitable for wall climbing

features include headlamp holders consisting of elastic straps or some kind of plastic knobs that hold it securely in place, easy-to-use adjustment dials for fit, and removable ventilation tabs to help control temperature inside the helmet.

ROPES

Rope, perhaps the most important tool in climbing, has evolved from hemp to high-tech. Choosing the right ropes for the job is very important: there are many choices to make, from the lead line to the tag line, according to the kind of climb you're doing. In almost all wall-climbing endeavors, you'll need one dynamic lead line and one static tag (haul) line. Or you can use a

dynamic rope as your haul line instead of a static rope; insurance should something happen to your main lead rope. Having two ropes ensures that you'll be able to retreat without having to do extra rappels, and they serve as a haul line and lead line combination. There are many combinations of rope to choose from; make your decision based on the length, difficulty, environment, duration, and style of climbing you're going to do. However, most big walls are climbed with a fatter lead rope for safety and peace of mind.

Lead line. For almost any big wall that requires aid climbing, fixing of ropes, hauling, and jumarring, a 60- to 70-meter dynamic lead rope 9.7–11 mm in diameter is best because it holds more falls than thinner ropes, is more abrasion resistant, and will stand up better than thinner ropes to the abuses of wall climbing. Some modern routes have been established with a 70-meter rope, so reaching their belays with a rope shorter than 70 meters may be impossible. Always check to see whether you need a longer rope before going on a climb. A rope with a dry treatment will resist absorbing water, boosting its performance and durability and prolonging its life; dry treatment rope is a good choice to have on a wall because it is liable to get wet. It's best to use a lead rope that holds at least 10 falls, has good handling characteristics, and has a low-impact force rating.

Tag or haul line. A tag line, also called a zip line or a haul line, is a mandatory piece of gear on a big wall. It's used for hauling the bags of gear, for pulling up extra gear the leader might need on a pitch, and for rappelling. Your tag line should be of the same length or longer than your lead rope, and it can be either a dynamic or a static rope. If you don't mind a little extra weight, using a longer tag line is useful for zipping up gear while on lead; it can be clipped in short to the haul bag, with the remainder being used as a lower-out line when hauling a traverse or pendulum. A static rope works better than a dynamic rope because there's no stretch or bounce when hauling, so it will last much longer. If you use a static rope, choose one that's 7–9 mm in diameter. Anything smaller tends to tangle badly, wear out faster, and snag on flakes and in cracks and is too small for safe rappels.

Anything bigger is heavy and cumbersome. If you use a dynamic tag line, choose one that's 9–11 mm in diameter. Advantages of using a 7–9 mm haul line are lighter weight and easier stacking and coiling. The advantage of using a 9–11 mm dynamic rope is that you have a backup lead rope and you can rappel and jumar easier on it than on the 7–9 mm rope.

Other options. If you plan on doing a wall that involves mostly free climbing and you won't be hauling a bag, consider using a 9.2–9.7 mm dynamic rope paired with a 7 mm tag line for rappelling, because this is a lighter setup. Another alternative is to use double or twin rope techniques, in which you clip the ropes alternately or together to create an efficient way of climbing with two ropes, which has the advantage and safety of having two ropes rather than one. If you are planning on doing an alpine wall that requires hauling, consider using a 9.7–10.2 mm lead rope and a 7–8 mm haul line.

BELAY DEVICES

Numerous belay devices are available today, and they all work well. Some of the many options to choose from include the GriGri, the Cinch, the stitch plate, and the figure eight. All these devices, including the GriGri, require that you always have your hand on the braking side of the device. The advantages of using a GriGri or Cinch are their ability to hold a climber once they're loaded without your hand constantly holding the tension and their ability to be used on a fixed rope as a locking rappel device. The other belay devices require you to hold the rope

Belay devices: belay plate that can be used to autolock belay; GriGri, belay plate with friction notches; tube device

Figure eight

Münter hitch

with your brake hand all the time that a climber is hanging on the rope. The advantage of using a nonlocking device is that you are able to absorb more force in a fall by allowing more rope to slowly pass through the device as the climber reaches the end of the fall, which helps when you're trying to keep forces lower while on difficult aid pitches. The Münter hitch is a belay technique that uses only the rope passing through a locking carabiner. This is not used much because it can twist and kink the rope, and it can be difficult to remember how to use it properly.

SLINGS, QUICKDRAWS, AND CORDELETTES

Carry eight to 10 shoulder-length slings on any wall climb. There are various materials and widths to choose from, but sewn slings that are 9/16 inch or smaller, and made of Spectra, are best. Slings are used to extend the clip-in point on any piece of protection to help minimize rope drag, to direct the rope away from edges or flakes, and to minimize a placement from dislodging itself.

A quickdraw, a sewn piece of webbing 4–6 inches long with a carabiner clipped to a loop on each end, is very useful for clipping in to bolts, stoppers, or fixed protection. Carry at least 10 on a big wall.

You'll need two cordelettes on any wall climb, one for each belay as you rotate leads. A cordelette is made of 7–8 mm cord cut in a 30-foot section and tied in a loop

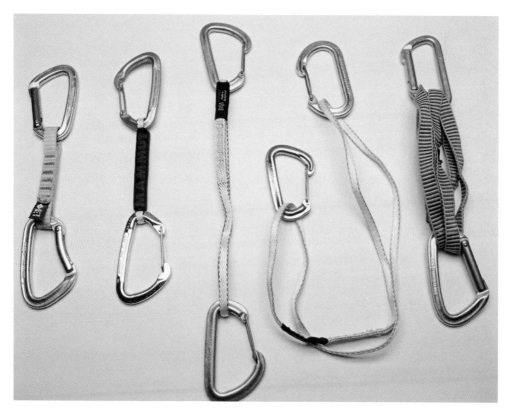

Various quickdraws (from left): standard; wiregate; medium length; shoulder length; doubled-over shoulder length.

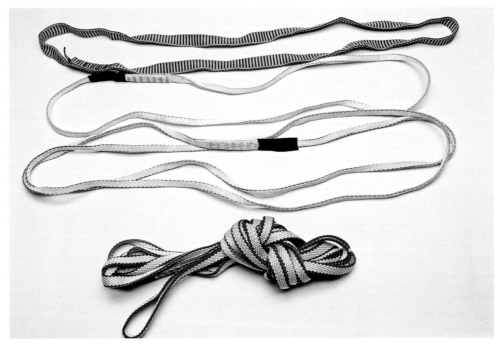

Cordelettes (from top): shoulder length runner; lightweight shoulder length; double length; sewn cordelette

with a double fishermans knot. To carry this lengthy piece of rope, double it over twice and tie it in an overhand knot clipped in to a locking carabiner on your harness.

CARABINERS

Oval carabiners work best for racking stoppers, pitons, and copper heads; they should also be used with your etriers because they're easier to grab and pull on than wire-gate carabiners. Wire-gate carabiners are the lightest carabiners available; however, any carabiners will work for racking the rest of the equipment.

A wall climb requires roughly 50 carabiners. On most wall climbs, eight to 10 locking carabiners will be necessary for fixing ropes, belaying, jumarring, and rappelling and for the haul bags and portaledge. Auto-locking carabiners are quick and handy; the twist-screw lock type is the safest.

SHOES

Wall shoes once consisted of Chuck Taylors or an old pair of hiking boots—they lacked function and design but were considered *de rigueur* back in the day. Modern wall shoes, which feature sticky rubber, narrow

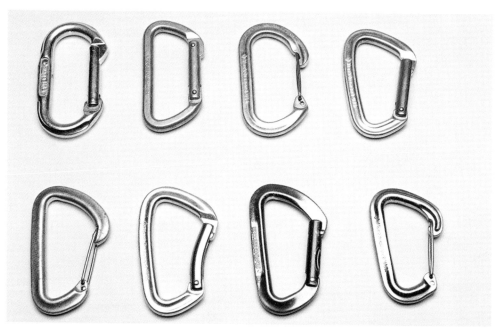

Various carabiners (from top left): standard oval; d-shaped; wiregate oval; pear shaped; wiregate pear; bent gate; keylock pear; small wiregate

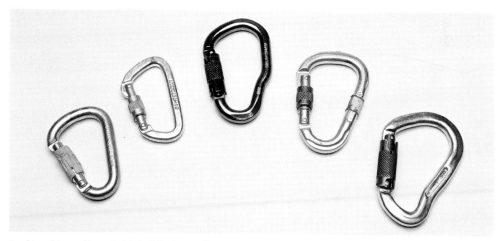

Locking biners (from left): ball lock; small screw lock; auto-lock; large screwlock; large auto-lock

profiles, flat edging capability, and style, are more comfortable than a pair of ratty old tennis shoes.

Your shoes are one of the most important tools on a big climb due to the amount of time you spend standing and climbing in them. A stiff-soled, sticky-rubber shoe that's either low- or mid-cut with laces is the most commonly used shoe for long aid routes. Having a pointy toe box is helpful for stepping in and out of the aiders, and some shoes now have a partial flat edging sole for stepping on edges, which are good for easy free climbing. Don't go on a wall in a pair of shoes that will fall apart halfway up; you need closed shoes that will stand up to a lot of rubbing against their front and sides. You need reliable footwear, and many companies make excellent shoes for wall climbing.

An alternative is to use a pair of comfortable free-climbing shoes you can stand in all day. A pair of high-cut lace-up free-climbing shoes give you greater precision when stepping in and out of aiders; and when you are ready to step out of the aiders and start free climbing a section, you'll have excellent friction and precision, which gives you confidence that you won't slip off edges or not be able to jam a crack as well.

Unless you're doing a route that has more free climbing than aiding, stick with comfortable wall shoes. If you're heading up on a pure aid climb that will require you to stand in aiders the whole way, avoid free shoes.

HAMMER

A good hammer is a vital tool on a wall climb. A wall hammer should have good weight distribution between the head and the handle for positive swing, a solid tie-in point at the bottom of the handle for an over-the-shoulder sling clip-in point, a hole on the side opposite the hammer head big enough to clip in carabiners for cleaning

Wall hammer

purposes, and a head weight of at least 18 ounces. Some hammers have a pointed end that is great for copper heading (see Basic Aid-Climbing Skills and Techniques later in this chapter) and cleaning.

You have a choice between a fiberglass handle or a wood handle. I prefer wood, because it tends to vibrate less, but it can break or crack if used improperly. The advantages of a fiberglass handle are that it won't break and if it gets wet the handle won't be slippery because fiberglass handles usually have a rubber coating. One way to make either type of handle easier to hold is to dip it in an all-purpose grip solution that dries quickly. This is easily found at a hardware store. Another solution is to wrap tennis-racket tape around the handle or use athletic tape wrapped in a spiral over the handle, and then wrap a few strips of tape over that for a hockey-stick feel.

PROTECTION

Pitons. Basically metal spikes for driving into rocks for protection, pitons (also called pins) have been used around the world for

Various pitons (from left): Lost Arrow #1; Lost Arrow #2; Lost Arrow #3; Lost Arrow #4; 1" angle; ³/₄" angle; ½" angle; sawed-off angle; #1 blade; #2 blade; #3 bugaboo; #5 bugaboo; pecker; birdbeak

more than 50 years. Until the 1960s, pitons were made of soft iron that would bend to fit in rock cracks for secure placement. These can still be found occasionally on routes and are usually left as "fixed" gear, but you should inspect these before trusting them as a safe placement. These soft-iron pitons have been replaced with stronger, more durable pitons made from forged steel or chrome-moly that can stand up to repeated placements and abuse. Many types of pitons are available today, and the best way to get to know their names, sizes, and uses is to go to your local climbing shop and get the clerk to show them to you. All pitons come in numbered sizes, and it's wise to learn these so you have a working knowledge of what you need and can call for them by number from your belayer if you need more gear while on lead. Pitons fall into three categories:

1. **Angles:** Wedge-shaped pitons, angles are one of my favorite pitons because they're reliable, they're durable, and they place relatively easily. This category also includes the Z-angle.

2. **Knifeblades:** Straight pitons that vary in length and width, blades are my favorite piton, and you will probably use them more than any other piton on your rack. Knifeblades come in six sizes. The most frequently used sizes are the thin-medium to long-medium sizes and

Various angles (from left): bong; ½" angle; sawed-off 1" angle; 1" angle; titanium channel angle; old ring angle

Two different-size Leeper Z-angled pitons

An assortment of Lost Arrows and knifeblades

the Bugaboos, the thicker version of the blade. The Lost Arrow, created by John Salathe to climb Lost Arrow Spire in Yosemite National Park, is the most durable piton but also the heaviest. A full rack of Lost Arrows (also called LAs) feels like a ton of iron but is worth its weight in gold when needed. The larger, thick LAs aren't used as much these days because camming devices and other tools work better. Check the gear requirements of your intended route, and if you're uncertain, throw a couple LAs on your rack just in case.

3. **Micropitons:** Very short and thin pieces of metal for the smallest seams and cracks, small pitons include the RURP (realized ultimate reality piton), a revolutionary piton created by Yvon Chouinard; birdbeaks (also called beaks), another revolutionary piton, created by John Middendorf; and peckers, another micropiton for thin nailing.

Hooks. There are several types of hooks to choose from, so be sure to match the best-looking hook for each placement. Obviously, a tiny hook on a huge flake won't work well, and vice versa. A lot of manufacturers make great hooks, but I've modified some of them to suit my needs.

Micropitons (from left): small toucan; wedge mallard; birdbeak; pecker; RURP

Micropitons (from left): large pecker; medium pecker; small pecker; birdbeak; RURP

Various hooks

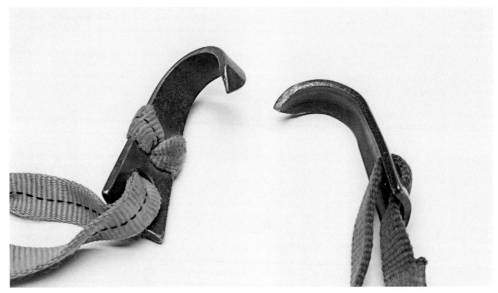

Customized hooks

Standard assorted hooks

Filing some hooks to a point helps keep them in place on small nubbins and edges. A good selection of four or five hooks will do for most walls. Some walls, such as the ones in Zion National Park and the deserts of the Southwest U.S., are made of sandstone, on which hooking is not very easy because the hooks cut through the stone and break its edges. A pointed hook is really bad for these kinds of routes; file the hook to a dull edge to help prevent this from happening.

Copper heads. Five sizes are commonly used, including the circle head for horizontal placements. Of these, the most common are No. 2s and No. 3s. These tend to work

Copper heads and tools (from left): center-punch; cold chisel; aluminum and copper heads

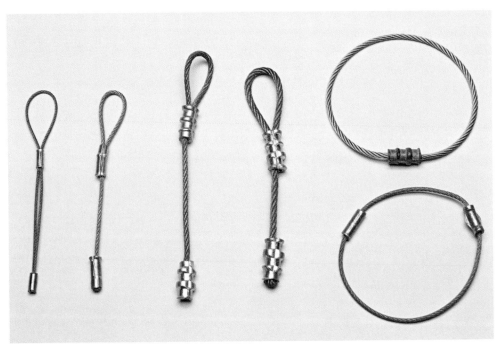

Aluminum circleheads

the best in most situations. Most aid aficionados make their own copper heads because you can customize them by adding an extra swage and make them as long or short as you want, but you can also buy them in a well-stocked climbing shop. Most heads are made of aluminum ferrules, but there are copper ones too. The copper ones are harder to place because the metal isn't as soft, but if you get a bomber copper head placement, it holds better than the aluminum. I usually go with the aluminum ones, and on the smallest size I usually double up the ferrule so I get more bite on the rock.

Clean aid tools. Cams, Tri-cams, slider nuts, cam hooks, stoppers, brass wires, Big Bros, and hexes provide bomber placements while saving the rock from damage. These days there are cams that fit into most pin scars, and there are even hybrid cams that have two different sizes of cams on the same unit, perfect for flares or pin scars. Some new devices on the market have made clean climbing even easier. Slider nuts are designed to fit into pin scars and thin cracks by a sliding mechanism.

Another simple clean device is the Leeper Cam Hook, a simple metal hook that comes in a variety of sizes, fits into various cracks, and works by simply

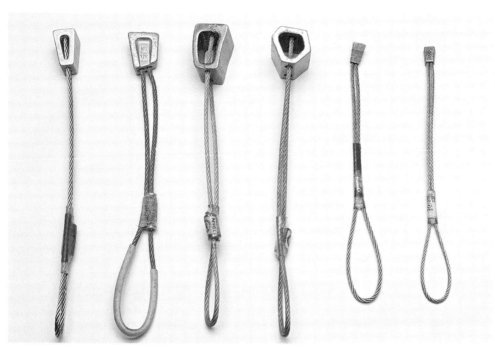

Various nuts

Three sizes of cam hooks

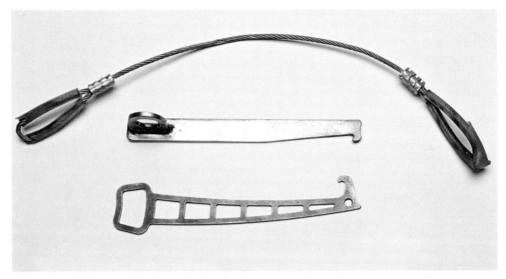

Cleaning tools (from top): funkness device; titanium nut tool/long blade; standard nut tool

camming against the sides of the crack under body weight. A good selection of stoppers and brass wires can get you up almost anything, and they're great to leave as protection if you are limited on cams. A Big Bro is a telescoping tubular device that uses a camming/wedging action to create secure placements in cracks 2³⁄₄–18 inches wide. It can be placed with one hand. Hexentrics, a bomber, lightweight alternative to camming devices, are ideal for doubling up on sizes covered by your cams. Hex placements can often be more solid than cams. Hexes don't "walk" and can fit into shallower pockets than cams.

Funkness device. This 2-foot-long piece of ⁵⁄₃₂-inch cable swaged with a loop at each end is used for testing and cleaning piton placements.

ETRIERS AND DAISY CHAINS

Etriers. Also called aiders, these are the most important tools you'll use when aid climbing, so spend a little more on a quality set for peace of mind. There are several setups, and some work better for different types of routes. The standard setup consists of two pairs of etriers, one for each daisy chain, and each consisting of four to five steps. Aiders that also have substeps in the second and third steps are the best, because they give you greater versatility when you are high-stepping. There are two kinds of aiders: alternating steps and straight steps. The straight steps usually have a spacer bar at the top to keep the steps open. Try each kind before you buy so you can decide which suits you better.

If you are new to aid climbing, get a

comfortable pair: each step is made of a wide strip of webbing with a stiff wire, which makes it easy to get your foot in and out of the aider. Lightweight aiders, which are more for alpine or speed climbing, tend to be uncomfortable on the arches of your feet over long periods of time. Be sure that there is a 4- to 6-inch grab loop at the top of the aider, because that's what you hold onto as you step up; it is also a good intermediate clip-in point.

Daisy chains. These are your main

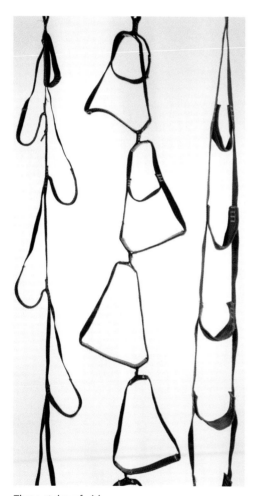

Three styles of aiders

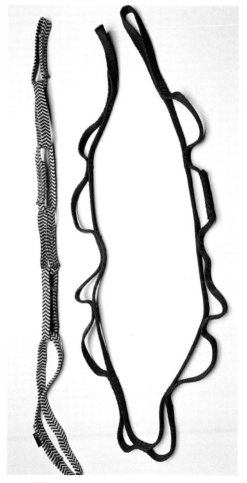

Two different daisy chains

tools when clipping in to belay anchors or pieces of gear while aiding, and they are invaluable on a wall. Daisy chains are 4- to 5-foot-long sewn loops of webbing with multiple clip-in points; there are several types made of various lengths, materials, and widths, and all are excellent. Choose a pair (preferably from the same manufacturer that made your aiders) which are each as long as you can reach overhead with the daisy chain girth-hitched to your harness. They don't need to be much longer, if at all, than your reach, and longer lengths just add excess bulk and weight. A few types work by pulling a length of webbing through a cam buckle; these are much faster and easier to use but may wear out more quickly.

Fifi hook. You need either a fifi hook or what I call a quickclip. A fifi hook is a small metal hook girth-hitched to your harness. A quickclip is a loop of webbing about 4–6 inches long with a carabiner at

Quickclip girth-hitched in short to tie-in point

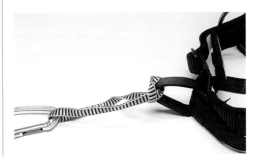

Quickclip girth-hitched to belay loop

Typical fifi hook

Quickclip girth-hitched to belay loop with extra biner on loop for short clip-in point

the end. Either a fifi or a quickclip can be used to attach your harness to each piece of protection as you move up.

JUMARS

Jumars, also known as ascenders, are mechanical devices designed to clip on and off the rope for climbing up the rope. There are many brands to choose from. They all work by means of a camming device with teeth on it, which clamps together the rope and the device while under weight and slides in only one direction. You need these to ascend the rope for cleaning a pitch, for ascending a fixed rope, and for hauling. For most wall applications, you'll want a pair of jumars with a large, comfortable handle and an easy-functioning camming mechanism that can be operated with one hand for optimal performance, speed, and safety (try it out in the store before you buy). Some

have handles, some don't. Examples of ones that don't have handles include the Petzl Tibloc, Wild Country's Ropeman, Petzl's Croll, and the Gibbs ascender.

Most ascenders work on almost any diameter rope down to 6 mm but are not recommended for anything smaller, while some work only on ropes of certain diameters (the Tibloc, for instance). The ultralight ones, the Tibloc and the Ropeman, work by mechanical advantage: a locking carabiner pinches the rope onto the teeth. In a pinch, you can use one of the multipurpose devices, such as Petzl's GriGri, Traxion, and Mini Traxion, as a jumar.

In the past few years, new designs have been developed using a very small camming device in tandem with a locking carabiner to perform the same function, but they are much smaller and lighter. Their advantage shines on a light alpine ascent or

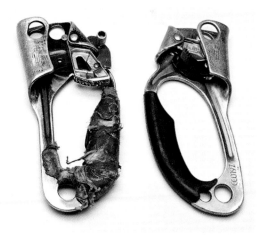

Three styles of jumars

when you don't plan on doing much jumarring. The disadvantages of these are that they are much harder to hold and they take a lot of time to take on and off the rope to pass a piece of protection or maneuver with while cleaning a pitch.

An alternative to jumars is a prusik knot. This is very time consuming and takes more practice to master than the jumar. For a prusik knot, you need a 4-foot length of 6–7 mm cord (to learn to use one, see Following in Chapter 2, Basic Wall-Climbing Procedures).

BELAY SEATS

On the wall, there aren't too many places to stand except for the occasional ledge, so having a belay seat can be a savior. If you are up on a wall without a belay seat, you can use your aiders as a makeshift seat by clipping in each end and slinging them under your butt.

You can make or buy a belay seat. Various models are available for purchase, from a plywood-type seat to a simple nylon belay seat. To make a belay seat, use a $^3/_4$-inch plywood panel cut to a size you like (Figure 1a shows 9 inches by 18 inches) with a $^3/_8$-inch hole drilled at least an inch from each corner. Use two 6-foot-long pieces of either $^9/_{16}$-inch webbing or 6–7 mm cord, each piece drawn through the two holes at one short end of the plywood and tied together with a double-fishermans knot; when these two pieces are drawn up above the plywood, they will extend $2^1/_2$–3 feet above it and form your clip-in point (see Figure 1b). Glue or tape

A5 belay seat

some $^1/_4$-inch-thick closed-cell foam onto the seat for comfort, and you're all set.

HAUL BAGS

The haul bag serves as the main transportation for all your gear on the wall. These bags have evolved from a potato sack to today's vinyl technology, multifunctional tools that can be carried as a pack for approaches and descents and are sleek and snag-free for vertical hauling. Today there

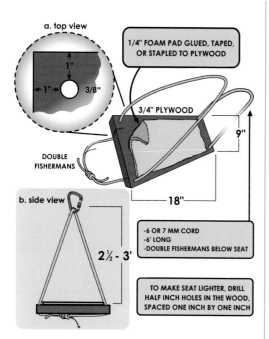

Figure 1. *Plywood belay seat: a, top view; b, side view*

A typical haul bag

are many different sizes to choose from, with a wide range of functional features built in for any and every wall endeavor.

Carrying harness. The old-school haul bag simply had two carry straps sewn on that made it feel like you were carrying a bag of rocks with shoulder straps made of fishing line. This type of bag was uncomfortable and usually had to be thrown away after use on one wall. Today's functional harness systems allow you to carry your haul bags to the base and down from the top in comfort. These harnesses also stash easily into a pocket designed into the bag for snag-free hauling and protecting the straps from abrasion. Padded shoulder straps are a must for larger bags because you'll be carrying a lot of bulky weight; be sure there is a sternum strap, top-load tension straps to secure the load, and a removable padded waist belt that you can stash inside the bottom of the haul bag while you're climbing. Some haul bags today have adjustable torso systems; others are fixed in place. Make sure the bag fits your torso because a bag that's too big will topple over and could be very uncomfortable to carry.

Materials and construction. Most haul bags are constructed from tough 33-ounce vinyl; however, there are also barrels designed for hauling up walls and some waterproof plastic welded haul bags for ultrawet conditions. The barrels are crush- and leakproof, great for storing food or items that need to stay dry (see also Haul Buckets at the end of this section). Most haul bags feature a grommet drain hole in the bottom, riveted or sewn seams that are doubled over to protect the stitching, and a coated nylon river-bag-style roll closure or double-wall draw skirt for durability. Compared to the skimpy bags of old, these

KEY EXERCISE: ORGANIZING YOUR GEAR

Organization at the belay will greatly enhance your efficiency and prevent frustrating, messy rope tangles and clusters of gear. With all the gear you need on a wall, it's a good idea to have it organized. Practice using these techniques:

- **Use a rope bucket:** Stacking your rope into a nylon bag is the best way to keep your rope tangle free and out of the way. Have one for each rope so you don't have to untangle the rope or remove knots while the leader is pulling for slack.
- **Stack the rope:** If you don't have a rope bucket, stack the rope on your haul bag, in a sling, or in one of the steps of an aider. Or you can tie a large loop in the end of the rope and stack the rope there.
- **Rack protection separately:** Use separate slings for cams and stoppers, pins, copper heads, and hooks to make it easy to pull off what you need without having to dig through a mess of gear.
- **Bag the gear slings:** I like to put all these gear slings into a large stuff sack that I keep in the top of the haul bag for easy access. On a longer wall, I like to have a small haul bag for gear only; this way, it's easy to find the gear whenever I need to put it away or pull some out.
- **Clip the gear slings:** You can clip gear slings in to the haul point, under the haul bag, or to the straps of the haul bag if the bag itself is full.

can stand up to repeated abuse and should last a long, long time.

Features. To discourage you from just throwing all your gear into a haul bag, creating a cluster of tangled gear, today's bags come with some key features for organization, smooth and safe hauling, and easy clip-in points. Some bags come with a dual-length clip-in haul point; others have same-length handles for the clip-in point. Two lengths allow you to clip the haul bag to the anchor using only the longer one, leaving the shorter one unclipped to allow for easy access to the bag. Handles on the sides and top of the bag make lifting and maneuvering it easier and also are a convenient place to clip gear for organization. Other nice features to look for include an internal zip pocket(s), preferably made of clear vinyl for easy viewing of contents, and an internal daisy chain that can be removed by a releasable buckle—this provides quick access to organized gear, yet keeps it stowed in the bag during hauling. Double haul loops under the bag are useful for clipping in another haul bag, portaledge, rain fly, water bottles, or whatever you want to have handy.

Sizes. Many different sizes of haul bags are available, starting around 1500 cubic inches and going to upward of 9000 cubic inches. Here are a few ideas on picking the right one for each route. For day outings, a smaller bag or haulable stuff sack works well to carry water and a few other items. For shorter walls—say, two to three days—one small bag and one medium bag would suffice. For weeklong walls, bring one to two large haul bags, because it's better to have two bags that aren't loaded to the gills. This way, you can dig into them and find and remove stuff sacks and gear without having to unpack a carefully packed bag

An organized belay

and having to clip everything into your belay, which can lead to lost items and total chaos. It's also a good idea to have a small haul bag that contains personal items such as sunscreen, water, food, clothing, camera, and headlamp; this keeps them readily available without having to break open the big pig.

Haul buckets. For crushable items, such as crackers, bagels, cookies, fruit, or a camera, make a haul bucket. Use a 5-gallon plastic bucket with a tight-fitting lid, such as those available at hardware stores. Drill four holes near the top, opposite each other, and string a 2-foot length of webbing through each set of holes, tying a knot on the inside of each hole to keep the knot from abrasion on the rock. These two slings will form your clip-in point. Drill another hole anywhere near the top of the bucket and one in the lid, then tie a 6-inch length of the same webbing through both holes as a keeper sling for the lid. Clip the bucket under the haul bag to keep it from snagging on edges during hauling.

PULLEYS AND HAULING DEVICES

For hauling purposes, you'll need a pulley. Just about any pulley designed for climbing will work well. Petzl and CMI make pulleys that are used in combination with a jumar or prusik knots. To use a pulley and jumars, you'll need a 3-inch aluminum pulley with sealed bearings. These pulleys are very strong and have a large radius, making it easier to haul heavy loads than with smaller pulleys. The pulley should have a

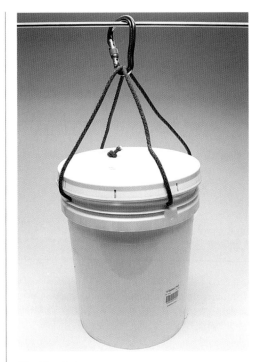

Haul bucket

Haul bucket open

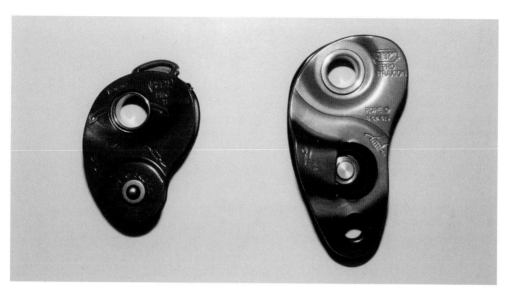

Combination hauling device

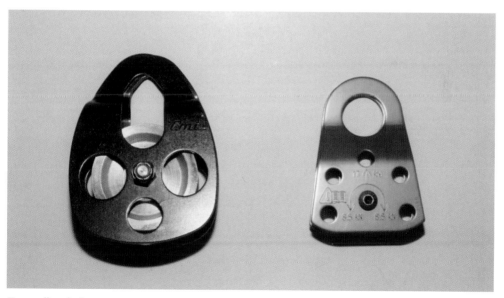

Two pulley designs

A swivel

large clip-in point. (Different hauling techniques and how to set them up are discussed in Chapter 2, Basic Wall-Climbing Procedures.)

Modern pulleys and hauling devices have made hauling setup time shorter and reduced the amount of gear needed. Several companies make hauling devices, including Petzl, Ushba, and Pika. Petzl makes the Pro Traxion and Mini Traxion and the well-known wall hauler; Ushba and Pika make similar wall haulers. These combo devices are faster and easier to set up than a pulley and two jumars or prusiks; invest in one if you plan on doing much wall climbing. If you use one of these combo devices, follow the manufacturer's instructions for proper operation.

Smaller pulleys, especially plastic pulleys, don't work as well under heavy loads, but they are OK for light loads. Wild Country makes a simple plastic wheel that clips on to a biner for ultralight hauling. Some micropulleys work OK for small loads, but for a large load you should use one that can hold at least 2,000 pounds. Always bring a lightweight backup pulley should your main one break.

Petzl makes a swivel that is very useful on routes that have traversing pitches. The swivel prevents the bags from spinning the rope when lowered.

THE TEN ESSENTIALS

The ten essentials has evolved from a list of individual items to a list of functional systems that deserve space in every pack. A climber will not need every one of them on every trip, but they can be lifesavers in an emergency.

Navigation. Most wall routes have good climbers topos that show key features to help you identify where you are and where you're going, including possible or mandatory free-climbing sections. A climbers topo is a great tool to refer to if you're unsure about where to go. A climbers topo usually tells you how difficult each pitch is, shows generally where each pitch goes, and tells you what size gear you'll need, how many bolts there are, and how long the pitch is. Both leader and follower should have a topo of the route.

Tip: Copy the topo and reduce it to make it pocket-sized. Laminate the topo or cover it with clear packing tape on each side to make it tear- and waterproof. Finally, punch a hole in it and use a rubber band to girth-hitch it to your harness, or keep it in a zippered pocket for quick reference.

Sun protection. A small tube of sunscreen, sunglasses, and lip balm with sun protection are essential for when you're charred in the heat.

Insulation. If you and your gear get wet, the strength of your rope is reduced and you are more prone to hypothermia. If your gear is wet and the temperature drops below freezing, you're in a really bad situation. Always bring proper storm gear; consider the worst that could happen and be ready for it. If you're climbing in a remote area in the mountains, weather can creep up on you without warning.

Illumination. Another necessary item is a headlamp. You'll need this for nighttime when you're eating and setting up your bivy, for climbing at night, and for descending in the dark. There are so many on the market that it's beyond the scope of this book to go into detail about them. Your headlamp should work with AA, AAA, or a 4.5-volt flat battery, be water-resistant or waterproof, and have an adjustable headband and a pivoting head. Bring extra batteries and a spare bulb too. Some headlamps use halogen bulbs; these burn more power but are better if you have to climb at night.

First-aid supplies. A minimum of first-aid supplies should always be included on the gear list; avoid adding too much bulk to the load, but do not bring too little to do you any good in case of emergency. A bare-bones first-aid kit isn't a bottle of whisky and a good night's sleep. To put together a proper first-aid kit, you need to consider:

- Your medical expertise
- The location and environmental extremes of your destination
- The duration of the climb
- How far you'll be from medical care and the availability of a professional rescue
- The number of people the kit will support
- Any preexisting illnesses
- Weight and space limitations

The medical kit should be kept organized and in a convenient carrying case. Excellent newer-generation bags have clear vinyl compartments that keep out dirt and moisture. Most outdoor specialty stores sell compact and convenient first-aid kits that are affordable and well worth the money.

Below is a list of supplies you should always carry with you; you can improvise some of these with items you already will be carrying. This is a longer list intended for any wall adventure ranging from El Capitan in Yosemite National Park to an expedition-style climb for which you might be traveling abroad for weeks at a time. These items don't take up too much space and could save your life. If you need to, you can pare it down to save weight and space.

- Knife with scissors and tweezers
- SAM splint
- Small roll of duct tape
- Roll of athletic tape
- Resealable plastic bags
- Several sizes of adhesive bandages, including sterile strips for larger deep cuts
- Antibiotic ointment
- Sterile pads with Lydocaine for cleaning wounds

- Nonadherent sterile dressings for burns or blisters
- Molefoam or moleskin
- Epinephrine auto-injector to treat anaphylaxis
- Pain reliever such as Motrin or Tylenol
- Anti-diarrhea pills such as Imodium
- Hydrocortisone cream
- Oral rehydration salts
- Cold medicine
- Sleeping pills
- Broad-spectrum antibiotic such as Zithromax (good for travel)
- Antibiotic such as Trimethoprim or Sulfamethoxazole for urinary tract, kidney, ear, sinus, or bronchitis infection
- Eyedrops such as Visine or a topical antibiotic for eyes
- Dental filling material
- Altitude medicine (for climbing at high altitude)
- Safety pins

Wall climbing involves suffering in one form or another, but it's better to suffer through just the hard work rather than an injury. Because your hands will get beaten into a pulp, at a minimum bring anti-inflamatory and pain medicine, a small medical kit, a roll of tape, a small knife, and topical antibiotic ointment for cuts.

Fire. On a single-day climb, this might be simply firestarter and matches in case of emergency. On longer climbs, a stove is essential to heat up food, brew a hot beverage, and melt snow for drinking water. The butane cartridge type stove is easier to use than gas stoves. Today there are sleek, lightweight hanging stoves that pack so small it's not worth going without one. Be careful when cooking on a portaledge, especially when the rain fly is on, because nylon melts at a low temperature!

Repair kit and tools. At a minimum this consists of a pocketknife and some duct tape.

Nutrition. When you're wall climbing, you're burning 3,000–6,000 calories a day. It's hard to eat during the day because you're moving most of the time, so breakfast and dinner are your main meals, with snacks supplementing them during the day.

You need about 3 pounds of food per person per day. This weight depends on the kind of food you bring: dry food is lighter than canned food but requires more water and usually a stove to cook it. Canned food is more convenient but heavier and not as nutritious. Try to balance a combination of good quality with convenience. For more remote alpine walls where weight is a big factor, bring dry food and cook it with a stove.

A list of foods that works well for wall climbing is shown on the next page. For more information on nutrition, see *Climbing: Training for Peak Performance* and *Expedition Planning,* both by Clyde Soles, in the Mountaineers Outdoor Expert series.

Wall food is only as good as you make it. Be creative and search the grocery store for food that doesn't crush easily, has decent nutritional value (not tons of junk food), takes little preparation, and is comprised mostly of carbohydrates. A few cans of beer round out a day of wall climbing nicely. Use different-colored stuff sacks to organize your food by meals—for example, breakfast,

Breakfast	Lunch and Snacks	Dinner
Apples, oranges (they don't break)	Dried fruit, mixed nuts, trail mix	Canned pasta or similar (no stove); quick-cooking pasta dinners or similar (stove); add a can of tuna
Bagels with cream cheese, peanut butter, or the like	Bagel and cream cheese	Bagels with pâté, tuna, hummus, etc.
Instant oatmeal (stove)	Sports bar, sports gel	Crackers, cheese, sausage
Granola with canned fruit	Peanut M&Ms or the like (in small wide-mouth bottle for easy access and crushproof container)	Premade meals such as burritos or veggies and pasta (in Tupperware container); be creative
Granola bar or breakfast bar	Hard candy, gum, or similar for dry mouth, throat	Precut veggies (in resealable plastic bags)
Coffee, yerba mate, tea, hot chocolate, or whatever you prefer	Fig bars or similar	Noncaffeine tea or similar

lunch, snacks, dinner—so you know where all the dinner food is at the end of the day. Resealable plastic bags are perfect for food that needs to be used in portions. If you bring crushable foods such as crackers or cookies, use a haul bucket clipped under the haul bag (see Haul Bags earlier in this chapter).

Hydration. Finding or having enough water is one of the biggest problems on a wall because most walls don't have a reliable water source, which requires you to haul it. At about 8 pounds per gallon, it's a significant part of the load that can't be omitted. I've climbed walls without enough water and thought I'd never make it off. You can survive without food, but not without water. It's better to have more than less because you can simply dump water out if you know you won't need it.

The rule of thumb is a minimum of $1/2$ gallon per person per day. If it's hot or you're at altitude, you'll need 1 gallon per person per day. A sign that you're dehydrated is if your urine is yellow or darker; clear urine is a sign that you're hydrated. When you're dehydrated, your body doesn't function as well.

Carry your water in solid containers that won't break; never bring glass. Collapsible containers (Camelbaks, Dromedary bags, Platypus, etc.) are the best because they compress as you use the contents, giving you more room in the haul bag. Don't use gallon water jugs with flimsy lids because they leak and can even burst open, soaking everything as well as losing your water. Bottled water and sports drinks are fast and easy sources for hydration that help replenish electrolytes.

Plastic 1- and 2-liter bottles work great, are inexpensive, and have a long life. I've seen a lot of people wrapping these in tons of duct tape and attaching glorified clip-in leashes to them for protection and easy clip-in points. This works well, but it's overkill. If you must, what works well is a simple shoestring-size cord a few inches long tied around the lip of the bottle and taped into place. You can also use thin cord tied vertically around the bottle with a few wraps of tape to hold it in place.

I keep a water bottle in the top of the haul bag and drink it at the belay. If you need water when you're leading, either zip up a bottle on the tag line for a swig or use one of the new double gear slings that have a hydration kit built in for sipping as you climb. These are really handy on long leads and on long free routes that you plan on doing in a day. Clipping a quart water bottle onto the harness has proven to work well too.

Emergency shelter. A portaledge is the best shelter on a wall climb. If you are on a one-day climb and not using one, bring a belay seat and a bivy sack or space blanket.

CLOTHING

On a wall, you experience dramatic changes in temperatures in a short period of time. You might sweat hard on a pitch, then get a chill at the belay anchor when the wind picks up or in the shade in the afternoon. Most cliffs become windy as the day goes on, even if it's really hot at the base (or just looks it). Remember that storms can show up unannounced and can last longer than predicted, so always be prepared. Once you get wet, cold, tired, and dehydrated and have to make a retreat, things can get dangerous in a hurry.

Bring enough warm clothing and a change of clothing in case you get soaked. By bringing ample clothing and protection for the worst weather, you'll be able to either retreat or stick it out comfortably. You might be cavalier and always go light, with nothing to protect you, until you get caught. People have died from exposure, so bring the minimum you're comfortable with. Obviously you don't want to bring a down jacket up a south-facing wall in August in Yosemite National Park or just a T-shirt and shorts on the Diamond on Longs Peak in Colorado's Rocky Mountain National Park in winter.

Wearing cotton is not acceptable; it doesn't insulate when wet, and it dries slowly. Excellent synthetics that are designed specifically for climbing dry fast and are cut for climbing movements. Synthetics stretch and provide warmth even when wet. Wall climbing is abusive on your clothing, so choosing the right kind is essential. Schoeller fabrics are especially good because they're water- and wind-resistant, have good stretch, and have a long life when it comes to the abuses of wall climbing.

A midweight synthetic top with a zip neck (for regulating temperature) and a zip chest pocket (a convenient place for a topo, lip balm, and the like), along with a softshell jacket for cooler temperatures and stormy weather or wind, provide enough protection for diverse conditions. A Gore-Tex storm jacket that packs small is essential, no matter what. If you're in a colder climate, bring a synthetic parka for belaying and hanging out in the evenings and mornings. Bring a pair of durable, stretchy pants that won't limit movement and will dry quickly if they get wet. Features to look for include a few zippered pockets (a cargo pocket is great), a low-profile waistband, Velcro or drawstring pant leg cuffs (to keep out windy drafts), and reinforced knees and butt. Bring a warm synthetic hat and a pair of windstopper gloves too.

ADDITIONAL GEAR

Knee pads. These are good to have because you're constantly in contact with the rock. They are ideal for when you have to haul because your knees take the most abrasion during hauling. Slip-on knee pads work better than the kind with elastic straps with Velcro and they are more comfortable.

Gloves. Another nice piece of gear is a pair of leather gloves. You can buy a pair of wall gloves that have the fingertips cut off, a clip-in loop sewn in, and a Velcro closure for a secure fit. You can also make a pair for less money by buying a pair of garden or construction gloves at a hardware store and making these features yourself. Leather gloves are very useful for keeping your knuckles from getting bashed, for belaying and rappelling, and for handling ropes, gear, and anything else on the wall.

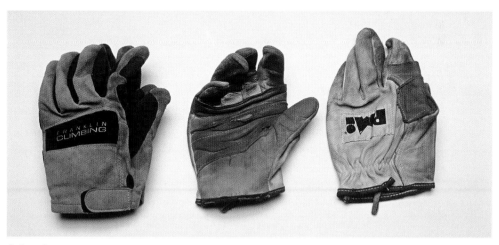

Belay gloves

PEE BOTTLES AND POOP TUBES

OK, now the filth: how do you deal with elimination while you're on a big wall climb? Urine is relatively easy to deal with: During the day, pee freely and away from the wall; use discretion when another party of climbers is below you. At night, pee into an empty water bottle and designate it as a pee bottle for the remainder of the climb. (It's much easier to use a pee bottle at night inside the portaledge than to deal with leaning out over it.) The Lady-J was designed for women's bathroom needs.

Excrement poses more difficulty. It's no longer acceptable to toss "mud" bags off the cliff or smear the walls. You need to use a poop tube. You can buy one, such as the new Metolius Waste Case, or make one out of PVC products found at a hardware store. Take a 12- to 24-inch-long length of 6-inch-diameter PVC pipe and glue a PVC cap to one end. At the open end, 4 inches from the top, drill two $1/2$-inch holes opposite each other; use $5/16$-inch webbing or 6 mm cord to tie a clip-in loop through the holes. Use a second PVC cap for a removable lid; drill a small hole in it to secure a keeper leash.

Whether you use a storebought or homemade poop tube, bring two or three plastic trash bags to line the tube. When you need to use the tube, you can either go directly into the inner bag or use a small brown paper bag and then toss it into the inner bag. If you're shy, hang a sleeping bag in the middle of the portaledge to act as a curtain. Sprinkle baking soda or lime into the bag with each use to keep the stench down and to keep the tube from exploding.

Now tie the inner bag shut, stuff it in the other bag(s), put it in the tube, and start laughing—because it's pretty damn funny. Clip the tube under the haul bag.

If the poop tube (either storebought or homemade) is too heavy for you, buy a roll-closure dry bag, such as ones used for boating, and use it for waste. Do your duty in a brown paper bag, then toss it into three garbage bags lining the dry bag. Roll the dry bag shut and clip it under your haul bag with a safe clip-in point.

When you are off the wall, dispose of all waste properly, such as at an RV dump station. A few years ago, a pair of climbers in Yosemite had put a toxic warning label on their PVC tube as a warning of its contents. When a tourist saw the ominous item in a dumpster, a call was made to the officials that there was a potential bomb in the park. After close inspection, it was determined to be a false alarm. I feel sorry for the ranger on duty that day.

BOLTING GEAR

It is usually a good idea to bring a bolt kit on a wall. A lot of routes can have a feature that breaks away, changing the route with every ascent and making it impossible to follow without adding a rivet or bolt to pass a now-blank section. Some old routes might not see much traffic, and the bolts may be too old and rusted to be safe. However, never add bolts simply because you're scared or can't do the climb. If you feel as though you can't do the route as it was originally intended, rather than adding a bolt, turn around and do the

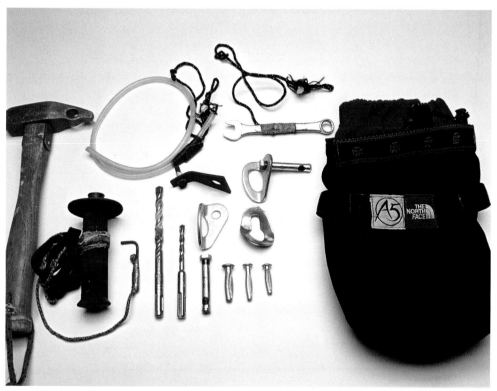

Typical bolt kit and bolt bag

route later when you have the ability.

A bolt kit includes a handle, two or three bits, a handful of bolts and hangers, a wrench to tighten bolts, and a blow tube to clean out the hole before placing the bolt. Obviously, you need to match the bolt size to the bit size. A $\frac{1}{4}$-inch bolt will be good for about 10 years, but if you have to drill, it's better to do everyone a favor by putting in a $\frac{3}{8}$-inch by $2\frac{1}{4}$-inch to 3-inch stainless-steel bolt with a solid new hanger. If you have to drill a bolt, make it a good one.

CHEATER STICK

There's a time and place for this necessary evil, but most of the time you don't need a cheater stick. A cheater stick is just that: a length of stick, tent pole, or whatever you want to use (light is best) that securely holds a carabiner at one end, which you clip in to a piece of fixed gear that's out of reach above you. A cheater stick up to 20 feet long has been used in the past, but for most purposes a stick 2–5 feet long is sufficient.

I think it's better ethically to climb without a cheater stick, which forces you to do *all* the climbing. However, if a short climber can't make the reach that was made on the first ascent and there's no alternative, a cheater stick works fine. A cheater stick is also helpful when a placement has blown out or broken to the point where there's nothing else usable and there's a fixed piece just out of reach.

GRADES AND RATINGS

Grades and ratings are important factors that describe a climb by telling you how long a climb normally takes, what level of difficulty it is, and what level of commitment is required. By understanding this information about the route, you'll be able to say, "Yup, I'm going to do that route" or "Man, that's way over my head."

The number rating given to a climb indicates its difficulty—or the difficulty of its hardest pitch, not necessarily the difficulty of every move or its continuous difficulty. The rating doesn't tell you all the information about a route, either. You won't learn if it's a thin crack, that it has a hooking section over a ledge, or whether an A3 section is an expanding wide crack through a roof. You'll get that information from the climbers topo of the route.

Ratings can also be somewhat arbitrary because a route can change over time with repeated ascents or as features break or become beaten out; ratings are definitely subject to change. Modern new-wave ratings have changed with advanced gear technology and climbers' attitudes, causing some old ratings to be different compared to today's ratings. For example, an old A4 rating would be considered modern A2.

These ratings are subject to interpretation and can be off target, so always use good judgment. Ratings are just a guideline and don't replace your knowledge and skills when you're out on the rock. Understanding the grades and ratings of a climb is a great launching point, and that is where I started my big-wall career. It's a fun process; there's a lot to talk about concerning commitment, ethics, and style in wall climbing. With experience, you'll begin to get a feel for it. These grades don't mean anything unless you have a solid respect for the stone and for yourself. I still learn things every time I go wall climbing. Above all else, have a good time and, as they say, practice makes perfect.

All climbs are rated according to the following categories:

- **Grade:** the amount of time and commitment level required
- **Class:** a broad difficulty rating ranging from hiking to free climbing to aid climbing to clean aid climbing
- **Seriousness:** the amount and quality of protection available on any climb

GRADES

A climb receives a grade to determine the length of time and the amount of commitment that a competent party needs to complete it. Grade ratings are open to interpretation because some parties are slower than others, and a strong party might be able to get up a grade V in half the time of a slower party. In general, grade ratings give you an idea of the amount of time you should expect to be on the route so you can plan accordingly. Used for both free and aid climbs, these ratings roughly outline the commitment necessary for an ascent.

Any grade can have a "+" added to it, which indicates that it requires a higher level of commitment, in regards to a higher free-climbing standard or aid standard, without increasing so much that it bumps up to the next grade level. By referring to the climbers topo, you can determine how fast you think the climbing will go according to the amount of hard climbing. Free climbing goes faster, so a grade V free climb will take less time than a grade V aid climb.

For example, the Astroman route in Yosemite National Park is rated grade V, class 5.11c. This climb, with difficult free climbing or some easy A0, requires a full day to climb for most parties. Now consider the Prow, of the same length and also on the same cliff, rated grade V, class 5.10a, A3. The Prow route takes most parties two days because of the amount of technical aid climbing. Both routes are rated grade V, but their actual duration is determined by free versus aid climbing. Look at another example of a harder free route of the same length on the same cliff: Quantum Mechanics, rated grade V, class 5.13-. It requires a higher level of commitment and will take

more time than Astroman, but not as much as the Prow.

As you can see, there are multiple levels within the grading system, so look at the climbers topo to determine how long the route should take. Once you start getting into grade VII, you're probably in a remote area in a foreign country doing a first ascent on a very big route. These routes require a long apprenticeship to understand the scope of planning, travel, expert all-around skills, and perseverance they entail.

Grade I: 1–3 hours

Grade II: 3–5 hours

Grade III: 5–8 hours

Grade IV: A full day

Grade V: One very long day to two days

Grade VI: At least two days and up to a week

Grade VII: More than a week in extreme conditions, alpine settings, and with difficult climbing

CLASS

The class of a climb is a broad description of its difficulty based on the consensus of the climbing community. The idea is to have routes across the United States feel the same for their level of difficulty, though this is not an exact science. Six classes are used to describe climbing types from walking to aid climbing.

Class 5 is subdivided into the open-ended Yosemite Decimal System, first created and accepted in the 1950s, which consists of a system of numbers describing the difficulty of a route starting at 5.0

(easiest) and currently ending with 5.15a. From 5.10 up, the numbers are subdivided further with the letters *a* through *d* to describe in more detail the difficulty of the climbing.

Class 6 is subdivided into the aid rating system starting with A0 and going to A6 (see Aid Ratings). The higher the number, the more uncertain the safety of placements becomes, with larger falls becoming more likely.

Class 1: Easy walking on trails

Class 2: More strenuous trail hiking on steep, rough terrain

Class 3: Scrambling that requires the use of hand- and footholds but doesn't require a rope; a slip won't turn into a fall

Class 4: Easy climbing that requires a rope and a belay using intermediate protection; a slip would result in a fall. Terrain can be climbed quickly, often resulting in simul-climbing

Class 5: More difficult free climbing using a limited number of hand- and footholds to ascend; requires a rope, a belay, and intermediate protection and takes more time to climb

Class 6: The available hand- and footholds are minimal to the point where the climber can no longer free climb and must resort to artificial climbing

Ratings will feel different on various types of rock and from area to area. At Indian Creek you might lead 5.10 and have no problem, but in Colorado's Black Canyon of the Gunnison, 5.10 will be different. Each climbing area has unique features and styles of climbing, and factors such as boldness, difficult routefinding, and hard-to-get protection will change the way a rating feels. Don't assume that because you climb at a certain level at one area, you can climb it anywhere. Our free-climbing rating system is limited and can be confusing. Use your judgment to determine if it's a route for you.

SERIOUSNESS RATINGS

In addition to the numbers of the Yosemite Decimal System, a suffix can be added to describe the seriousness of a fall or the availability of protection on a route. Sometimes routes get these seriousness ratings after the difficulty rating, and they should be attempted by only those with expert experience and solid judgment skills because a fall could lead to serious injury or death.

PG-13: A route that can be well protected with enough solid placements to avoid any serious fall

R: A route with sections on which it is difficult or impossible to get protection and on which there will be a runout between safe pieces of protection; a potential long fall could result in the leader suffering injuries

X: A route on which the protection, if any, is unreliable and hard to find, and the leader could take a serious or life-threatening fall

A route rated 5.11c R might require you to climb the crux while run out over good protection. If it were rated 5.11c X, it might mean you would be climbing the crux with the possibility of a fall with serious consequences.

These ratings can be misleading, however, because you don't always find the R or X section of a climb matched with the crux of the climb. For example, you might find on the 5.11c R or X pitch that, after you have climbed the well-protected crux of the climb, you have to climb a less-difficult section that has no protection or a fall potential that could be serious or deadly.

This phenomenon is created by the limits of our rating system. It's best to try to find more information about a route or talk to someone who's done the route before you try it to determine whether this is the case with its seriousness rating. If you can't find any local information, use your best judgment on whether you should climb the route. If your climbing ability is above what the climb is rated, you'll be able to climb runout sections within your ability. If your ability reaches to 5.11a, don't try to do a 5.12 R route without accepting that you'll probably fall off.

AID RATINGS

Aid ratings differ from free-climbing ratings in that they are determined by combining the route's technical difficulty with the potential of a leader fall. The rating system starts with A0 and goes to A6, which indicates an A5 pitch with an A5 anchor: certain death if you blow it.

A0 (a.k.a. French-free): Simple aid climbing on routes with a hard section that either has some fixed pins, bolts, or fixed gear or requires placing a solid placement and pulling on it to get through a short section you can't free climb; it doesn't require you to use daisy chains or aiders

A1: Requires using daisy chains and aiders and offers solid placements that are easy to place and will hold a considerable fall; cam, stopper, or pin placements are easy and straightforward to find and make; when placing anchors with natural gear, all pieces in it should be bomber A1 placements

A2: Refers to a solid placement that might be more time-consuming to place; a pin might have to be tied off or a cam might not be in a perfect parallel placement, but these will hold a considerable fall once properly placed; placements can include tiny stoppers, slider nuts, rivets, pins, or cams; the crux is usually a short section of insecure climbing above good protection and a safe fall

A2+: Requires the leader to have good equipment placement and routefinding skills, as well as to be able to climb for a longer section under marginal security, though there is no serious fall potential

A3: Requires the leader to have good equipment placement and routefinding skills, as well as the ability to place hooks, thin pitons, and other precarious equipment, to climb expanding or rotten rock and to be able to string a long section of marginal placements with a possible 50-foot fall, though such a fall is unlikely to result in serious injury

A3+: Has serious consequences in a potential 50-foot fall

A4: Requires the leader to possess excellent equipment placement and routefinding skills, as well as the ability to climb long sections on hooks, thin pitons, and other precarious equipment, to climb expanding and/or rotten rock, and to string long sections of marginal placements; there are serious consequences in a potential 60- to 100-foot fall

A4 + : Takes longer to climb due to tedious and time-consuming placements, leaving the climber to suffer through hours of anxiety and uncertainty; very serious consequences, including death, in a potential fall

A5: Pitches have no chipping or drilling; the entire pitch (except for belay anchors) consists of body-weight-only placements that won't hold a fall; a fall can be more than 200 feet and is certain to cause serious injury or death

A6: An A5 pitch that is led off of an A5 anchor. This is the most serious pitch of aid you can lead. If you blow a single placement you will rip out all the remaining pieces of protection in the pitch and then rip out the anchor. If you fall, you buy the farm

The aid rating system is evolving with modern practices, attitudes, and advancements in technology; today it has more room for interpretation than it did in the past. Part of this is due to repeated ascents of routes, placements getting beat out to the point where they no longer require pins, features falling off, and more-advanced equipment. What was once considered A5 on a first ascent in, say, 1975 may be considered new-wave A3 + by today's standards.

Any route can face these changes, which may require subsequent ascents using a chisel or drill to piece together a blank section or to find a new way up the route, for better or worse. Updates on routes are often noted in new guidebooks and at climbing shops nearest to the route. Some routes may have had only a handful of ascents or no repeats at all and may still maintain their original rating. Check online or with locals for information about a route in question before blasting off.

CLEAN AID RATINGS

Clean aid-climbing ratings are basically the same as aid ratings, but they use the letter *C* instead of *A*; in other words, A1 is C1, and so on. If a route says it's been done at C3 + , you might consider bringing two or three pins just in case something has changed; bringing a hammer can be helpful for tapping in stoppers for a better placement and for cleaning stuck gear.

BASIC AID-CLIMBING SKILLS AND TECHNIQUES

Once you familiarize yourself with the equipment and the ratings of aid climbing, the next step is to know how to place all these gadgets efficiently and with confidence so you can move upward. This section shows you how to get up the easiest as well as some of the scariest and hardest aid climbing possible, using techniques ranging from nailing expanding flakes and copper heading rotten corners to making A1 cam placements and tricky nut placements. This section discusses how to place different types of pitons and how to use hooks, copper heads, camming units, stoppers, and other clean aid-climbing pro in the process of making upward progress.

PLACING PITONS

Piton craftsmanship is a fading art form as advances in technology have given us clean aid-climbing devices such as slider nuts, microcams, and cam hooks, which have for the most part eliminated the need for hammering pitons. When I first started big wall climbing, I tended to overdrive pitons, but eventually I learned not to do this, saving a lot of time and damage to the rock. It may take some practice to learn how to place a secure piton without overdriving it or causing major damage to the rock, but with practice you'll have it down to a science.

When you drive a piton, it gives off an ascending ringing sound. By watching and feeling how well the piton is sinking into the placement and by listening to the sound, you will learn when to stop hammering. Getting familiar with the many types of pitons will help when you start to use them in different-size cracks, and it will teach you which piton works better than others for a particular placement. Once you are familiar with the different types of pitons (also called pins), you need to practice.

The key to any piton placement is reading the rock and determining what size piton you'll need. Once you've looked at the crack and felt the size with your fingers to help gauge what size piton you'll need, take a piton in that range and place it snugly in the crack, giving it a tap with your hammer to make sure it stays in place. Be sure it doesn't fall out, because if you drop something on a big wall, it's gone for good. You can usually tell right off if it's too big or too small: the best way to gauge this is to place the pin so it's about one-third to two-thirds of the way in the crack before you drive it. If it looks as if you can drive the pin so that it will make a good placement just as the piton's eye hits the crack, then you're ready to drive it; if not, try a different size.

When placing a piton under a roof, make

KEY EXERCISE: PLACING PITONS

Start by finding a rotten, worthless boulder, preferably with various cracks, on which you can practice. Make sure it's near your home, not at your bouldering area or on private property, which can lead to problems. Bring your hammer and pins, aiders, daisy chains, harness, a funkness device, and your helmet. Wear a helmet while testing your first pitons, because if a piton pops out, it could hit you in the head!

Angle placement before hammering

Angle placement after hammering

sure there will be enough room for your follower to clean the piton: leave at least 8 inches above the pin to swing the hammer, because otherwise it can be very difficult to clean this type of placement.

Before you start driving the pin, look at the edges of the crack for fractures, loose rock, and crumbling debris, which indicate how well the rock will hold up. As you drive the pin, listen for the ascending ringing sound that increases as the pin sets in the rock. If the pin bottoms out, the crack expands, or the rock breaks, the ringing will turn into a dull thud. Take the piton out and

find a better placement.

Once you've hammered the pin till it looks, sounds, and feels good, as though it's being restricted as it's driven and has a nice ring to it, give it a test. I've found that in soft rock, a solid-looking pin can fall out under a soft fall or a light test; in granite and other hard rock, a piton will bite more easily and generally requires less effort to place. There are three standard ways to test a pin:

1. The old-school method is to simply clip one end of your daisy chain to the piece, apply your weight slowly until it holds, then bounce vigorously.

This method takes a lot of energy, can cause you to create too much force and blow the placement, and is too time consuming.

2. Another method is to clip your aiders to the piece and slowly step onto the piece, hoping it holds—a time bomb–like effect that isn't too wise but is effective if you know it's a secure placement.

3. The best way to test a piece is with a funkness device. To do this, clip one end of your funkness device to the placement and one to the hammer and, using a downward swinging motion, give the pin a solid yank. This generates a force comparable to a fall and is the best testing method for all pin placements. Start with a light swing and build up to a solid yank on the piece unless it looks solid right off. Watch the pin during this test to see if it moves or if the rock breaks away, and be sure to keep your face away from it because it could pop out.

Should the pin move, use a different size or a better placement, but if it holds, you're ready to move on it.

Any piton that sounds good and passes the funkness test but is sticking out more than an inch from its eye will have to be tied off. This happens a lot when you're stacking pitons (see page 67). The best way to tie off a piton is to clove-hitch it as close to the rock as possible with $9/16$-inch tubular webbing. Tie a water knot in the webbing so that when it is clove-hitched around the

Using a funkness device to test a piton placement

pin, it is about 3–5 inches long. You can use a slip knot or a girth hitch for this purpose as well, but they're much harder to undo because they cinch down tight under weight, making them more difficult and time-consuming to retrieve. An additional tie-off can be added through the eye of the piton and clipped in to the rope as a leash in case the pin falls out.

Tied-off knifeblade with keeper sling

Tied-off angle without keeper sling

Angles. These are one of my favorite types of pitons because they are reliable and durable, and they place relatively easily. They're a mandatory piece on your rack, and with some practice, you'll be placing these with confidence.

Lost Arrows. Placing Lost Arrows is a lot of fun but, as with angle pitons, it takes practice not to overdrive them. The longer,

A Lost Arrow placement before hammering

A good horizontal Lost Arrow placement after hammering

An OK blade placement (but it would be better with angle on opposite side)

Best blade placement

Better blade placement

Tied-off blade

thinner LAs work especially well in expanding flakes and rotten rock because they provide more surface area, creating greater holding power.

Knifeblades. Blades are great for stacking with other pitons, perfect for thin expanding flakes, and bomber in horizontal placements—they can also be used as a cleaning tool, as an eating utensil, and even for spreading peanut butter on a bagel! Place a blade about one-third its length before driving it with a hammer. Knifeblades can be clipped in two different ways.

1. The eye that is bent to the side is best for most placements because it creates a camming action on the piton when a

force is created, making it hold better.

2. The second eye is best for horizontal placements or when it makes a cleaner clip-in point with the carabiner.

Place the blade with the offset eye facing the best direction for any given placement; in other words, a blade should be placed in corners with the offset eye facing away from the corner so when it's clipped, the force creates a camming action on the pin. Experiment with right- and left-facing corners to see how this works.

One thing to be careful of is overdriving blades, especially in expanding flakes, where blades tend to be very difficult to extract and might require a funkness device to remove. If a blade bottoms out before it's a solid placement, stop hitting it, because it could bend and weaken the piton. Be kind to your blades; repeated use causes them to break.

Micropitons. For microthin seams, you'll use small pitons such as RURPs, birdbeaks, and peckers. In a solid piece of rock, these pins hold amazingly well due to their hooking mechanism. Be gentle with the rock and watch how hard you swing your hammer because all these small pitons can bend and break, easily blowing out your placement. It's best to tap lightly with your hammer when driving them into the rock. Keep an eye on the rock around the placement to make sure it doesn't break or fracture, because you'll get only up to $3/4$ inch of bite in the rock. Once it looks as if it's going to be a solid placement, drive the hammer a little harder and bury the sucker!

Stay away from using your funkness device on these and do a light bodyweight bounce test instead. Do this by attaching a daisy chain and an aider to the piece, step down in the aider you're on until the daisy chain pulls tight on the upper placement on your harness, and carefully weight the piece. Give it a little bounce, and if it holds, keep moving up!

The RURP is the only micropiton to use in a horizontal placement because the others weren't designed for this purpose. They are mandatory for any wall rack, even if you bring just two.

Good pecker placement

Good birdbeak placement

Good horizontal RURP placement

STACKING PITONS

If you can't make a single piton work for a solid placement, you'll have to improvise, and there are many creative ways to stack or nest pitons. Combining two or three pitons can make effective "nests" that can accommodate most hard-to-get placements.

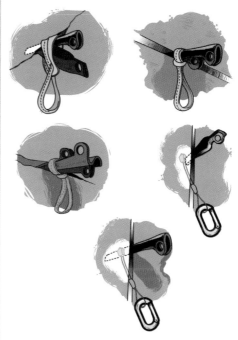

Figure 2. *Stacking pitons (from left): the standard X stack is the most effective way to fill gaps that are much too large for a lone pin; an inside stack works when one pin will almost fit; the Z stack offers the greatest range of stacking configurations; a pin-and-nut stack in shallow cracks eliminates a tie-off—and leverage; clean stacking keeps it sporty and preserves the rock*

Two Leeper-Z pitons

Any nesting combination should be designed to hold a downward pull and usually needs to be tied off.

When placing two pitons, it's best to hand-place the larger one first and hammer in the second (see Figure 2). When placing three pitons, it's best to place the third piton between the first two to create the best expansion. One piton designed specifically for this is the Leeper Z, a piton shaped like a Z that is designed for stacking (see Figure 2). You can also stack a pin with a stopper by holding the stopper in place while driving the pin in next to it (see Figure 2). Experimentation is sometimes the best way to get the job done.

HOOKING

Hooking is probably the scariest aspect of aid climbing. To overcome this fear, practice hooking, but *never* practice hooking on a free climb.

The best way to test a hook is to carefully weight it using your aiders. I always test hooks by stepping in the bottom step of the aider attached to the hook so I'm still below the piece I'm standing on, especially if it is also a hook. This prevents a shock load from causing the piece I'm on to pop off. I almost never bounce-test a hook because it can jiggle loose between bounces, causing it to pop off. While testing the hook, look at it from the side, not

---

KEY EXERCISE: HOOKING

Practice hooking up creaky flakes, microedges, and crumbling slopers on a small boulder, using different hooks to get a good feel for how they work and don't work. Start on the scrappy boulders you use to practice placing pitons, and bring a selection of hooks to try on different-size edges.

A good filed hook on a flat edge

A good standard hook on a big edge

Placing a hook

Step in the lower step to test a hook placement.

Slowly test the hook with your face averted.

Walk up the aiders while watching the hook.

Clip in to the hook at or above chest height to scout the next placement.

straight up at it, because when hooks pop off, they come off hard and fast—a helmet is a very good idea here.

When the hook is holding all your weight and you feel good about it, carefully move up the aiders to the second or third step and clip in to the hook with either a fifi hook or your daisy chain. Make sure the sling tied to the hook isn't too long, because 3 extra inches of reach could be everything you need; usually about 2–4 inches below the hook is about right.

Once you start on a long hook section, it's better to try to finish it because down-hooking is much more difficult. If you have to down-hook, climb down to the bottom steps in the aiders so it's easier to transfer to the next hook below you. Trying to get back on a hook when you're too far above it can cause it to shift out away from the rock.

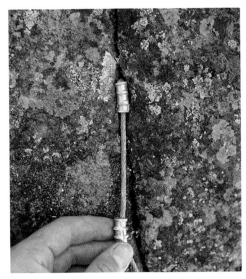

Find the best-fitting copper head before placing it.

COPPER HEADING

Most trade routes have some fixed copper heads, whereas more-difficult routes require you to do some copper heading of your own. Placing heads takes a fair amount of practice.

Select a head about the size of the placement or a little bigger, and hold it up to the crack to see if it's a good fit. If it needs a little flattening or shaping to fit the crack better, tap the head with the hammer against the rock and customize it before placing it. Take the head and tap it into place with the pointy end of the hammer till it holds. For horizontal placements, a circle head works best because it pulls on both sides of the placement, distributing

Custom fit the head to the placement before pasting it.

Tap the head into place.

Use a center-punch to fine-tune the placement.

Paste the top, bottom, and sides with the hammer.

Use a center-punch to fine-tune the placement.

the weight evenly. Place these the same as you would the other copper heads.

At this point, use a center-punch tool and start pasting the head into the placement as if you were spreading plaster into a crack. You can also use an LA to paste the head, but it's harder to hold while you're hammering. Start pasting the head near the biggest part of the crack and work around it till it looks solid. In really shallow placements, try to paste as much of it into the rock as you can, including pasting it on the side of the crack for maximum hold.

A common mistake is to test heads too hard, causing the cable to break away and blowing your placement. Never funk-test a head! This will almost always snap the cable, ruining your bomber placement and leaving the remains to block another placement. It's better to clip in to it and give it a bounce test instead, but be gentle

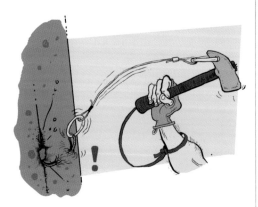

Figure 3. *The funkness device is so effective at cleaning gear that it can break the cable off a copper head.*

and go slow. When you're stringing several of these in a row, if you jerk-test one and it pops, you could potentially pull more! If it holds, get moving!

In most cases, it's better to leave copper heads fixed, because repeatedly placing and removing them causes damage to the rock, and if the cable breaks (see Figure 3), a subsequent party will not be able to use the same placement, resulting in further damage to the route.

MAKING CLEAN AID PLACEMENTS

In general, modern clean aid-climbing techniques are practiced to save the rock from total destruction, and this is a more efficient way of getting up, anyway. For most aid climbing, you'll use clean aid-climbing tools such as cams, stoppers, hexes, Tri-cams, Big Bros, brass wires, cam hooks, and slider nuts.

These are usually easy to place. Aid climbing requires you to have a placement that will hold simply body weight, rather than fall forces, so a lot of times you can get away with a more marginal placement than you would need for free climbing. This is true with placing cams, stoppers, and micronuts. There aren't too many tricks to these placements, so use your best judgement and if it holds, keep plugging away.

Slider nuts have a sliding mechanism that makes for easy placements. These are handy for speed climbing and to keep from hammering pins into trade routes. Be careful not to overstuff them into a crack, because they can be hard to clean after being weighted. They also have a tendency to get stuck in expanding flakes. If this happens, hammer a pin into the flake until it expands enough to extract the piece, then clean the pin.

Another simple clean device, the Leeper cam hook, is for bodyweight only! Stoppers and brass wires are always useful on the wall rack. In a pinch, you can always tap a small stopper into the rock to make a better placement.

PLACING PROTECTION IN EXPANDING CRACKS

On many routes, you might encounter an expanding flake or crack. These tend to make hollow ringing or thudding noises when beaten on with a hammer and can even flex under weight. There are a few things to consider when placing pitons in expanding flakes.

Because the flake or crack expands when a piece of gear is weighted, it's best to stay in the third step of your aiders while placing another piece higher because this creates less torque. Another consideration is that as you shift weight onto the piece you just placed, the piece you are already on might shift or pop out. To prevent a fall, it's best to keep your daisy chains clipped in to the piece you're on as well as in to the piece you're placing so that in case either placement fails, you're connected to the other one (see Figure 4).

Some expanding flakes require a piton to be hammered into them. Generally, take a large piton and drive it into the flake at the bottom of the expanding section to take out

Figure 4. *On expanding terrain, clip one daisy chain in tight to the piece you're driving, and you're covered if the piece you're on pops.*

as much of the expansion as possible. Then place each piton with a softer swing of the hammer than usual. By staying clipped in to the piece you're placing, you can periodically test it to see if it will hold. It's a delicate act; don't use a funkness device for testing. Instead, use your weight by standing in the aiders and doing a light bounce test. Check whether the piece above the one you're on widens the crack, because this may pop out the piece you're on, leaving you hanging on only the half-driven piton. If you think the piece you're on might fall out as you place the one above, hammer the upper piece hard and fast so it will hold. This is a skill that takes practice to develop.

One final consideration is that if you need to place only one or two pitons, it might be better to try using a cam hook if possible.

To clean an expanding flake, hammer the pitons back and forth a lot as the crack pinches them. Use a funkness device to clean stubborn pitons. One trick is to pull out on the funkness device with one hand and use the other to hit the piton up and down with the hammer. You can also hammer a bigger piton in near the one you need so the crack expands enough to free your original piton.

USING ETRIERS AND DAISY CHAINS

A typical setup for aid climbing includes girth-hitching both daisy chains to the belay loop on your harness, with one pair of aiders clipped in to a single carabiner at the end of each daisy chain. Set up each pair of aiders with one four-step and one five-step for more versatility. Use either a fifi hook or a quickclip to attach your harness to each piece as you move up.

With this setup, you're ready to learn how to move upward. Here is the typical process for using your aiders and daisy chains:

Above: *Place a piece at arm's reach.*
Below: *Clip in a pair of aiders and a daisy chain to the placement.*

1. With a single carabiner, clip one of your daisy chains and its pair of aiders to the piece of gear that you've tested (see Figure 5).

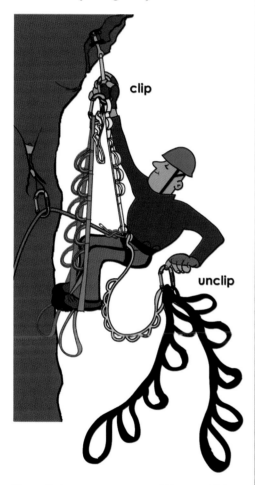

Figure 5. *As soon as you commit to your high piece, unclip your low daisy chain to prevent accidental shock loading should the high piece pull out.*

2. Grab the loop at the top of the pair of aiders, or the biner they are clipped to, place one foot in the fourth or fifth step, and put your weight onto it.
3. Walk your feet up this pair of aiders to the second or third step.
4. Using either a fifi hook or a quickclip, clip your harness in to the biner with which you attached your aiders and daisy chain to the piece of gear, then sit back in the harness.
5. After you've clipped your rope in to the piece of gear below, unclip the second daisy chain from it (see Figure 5) and either let it hang under you or clip it to your harness out of the way.

The next step is to look at the rock ahead and decide if you need to move up into the substeps or even the top steps to get the next placement. Almost all your placements can be made from the third or second step, unless you see a better placement higher up and decide it's worth the effort. If you do use the substeps or top steps, extend your clip-in point so you can reach higher. For the second substep, do this by clipping a biner directly from your harness belay loop in to the piece; for top stepping, extend the length of the clip-in point because your harness will be above it. This is a strenuous activity on a vertical wall and nearly impossible on overhanging terrain.

Once you get the next placement, repeat steps 1–5 till you reach the end of the pitch or a section that you decide you'll free climb.

Grab the loop and walk your feet up.

Then clip in to the piece with your quickclip.

Find the best piece and make the next placement.

Again, place your aiders and walk up them.

Clip in to the piece and keep repeating these steps.

You can also use your aiders for a rest: put your foot in a step, bend your leg, and sit on your foot. This takes the pressure off your waist and makes a good rest.

STEPPING OUT OF ETRIERS TO FREE CLIMB

On many routes, there are sections that you can free climb instead of aiding. To help in the process of switching from aid climbing to free climbing and back to aid climbing, use your climbers topo to help identify where you are and where you're going, including possible or mandatory free-climbing sections. Keep the topo in your pocket to refer to if you're unsure about where to go. If you need to step out of the aiders and start free climbing, here are a few things to consider.

- Because free climbing is much faster than aiding and in free climbing it's important for your belayer to pay close attention to your movements, tell your belayer when you're going to start free climbing.

- Another consideration is how difficult the free climbing looks and whether you're wearing the right kind of shoes for free climbing. Typically, on a hard aid route you are wearing comfortable aid-climbing shoes, but if you think you'll be alternating free-climbing with aid climbing, consider wearing a comfortable pair of free-climbing shoes for just this purpose.

- When you start free-climbing, make sure that you unclip your daisy chains and clip them out of your way.

- The most important thing to consider is where the route goes and what you're going to get for protection. Be sure you can see where you're going and that you can get in safe protection. Commonly what happens is that when the free climbing section is over, you'll have to place a piece of gear and clip in to it to start the aiding cycle over again. Keep communicating with your belayer so he or she knows what to expect, whether it's free climbing or aiding, tension on the rope or slack, etc.

PLANNING

When planning a big wall climb, you need to consider what route to choose, who your partner will be, and the amount of skill you and your partner have. You also must consider what season you'll climb in and a realistic amount of time for the climb according to its difficulty and your skill level.

CHOOSING A ROUTE

There are so many big-wall routes to choose from that picking the right one is daunting. You might have a route at the top of your list that is everything you want in a climb, but perhaps it is too advanced for your skills. You're definitely not going to waltz up a hard nail-up right off the bat. You can always bite off more than you can chew, but the rock will have the final say. Starting with a moderate climb will boost your ego while dialing in your skills so you can conquer the next wall up the scale. In big wall climbing, it's typical to build up your experience over time so when you do get to the base of your dream climb, it's no longer over your head.

To climb any wall, whether it's 1000 feet or 3000 feet, you need a solid foundation in rope handling, gear placements, tying and using multiple knots, belay techniques, jumarring skills, hauling setups, knowledge of aid climbing equipment and the process of aiding a pitch, multipitch procedures, and making solid, safe anchor systems. Being gung ho can get you into trouble if you don't have a solid working knowledge of these systems.

Each route is unique and commands respect. Stay within your limits so you can learn the systems and the process of wall climbing without the added stress of hard climbing. A moderate eight-pitch A1/C2 route that's mostly straight up without large roofs is a good place to start. A 1000-foot route is ideal because you can reach the top relatively quickly, but it's also easy to retreat from. You'll have a few days to dial in your systems and get comfortable hanging out up there without a heavy amount of stress.

Choose a route according to what you want to do. If you're into pure aid, find a route that has more aid and no free climbing. Do the opposite if you want to do more free climbing but want a few pitches of A1 or A2 to get a feel for what aid climbing is all about. Don't get onto something you're not going to have fun on.

An A2 route might seem comfortable until you have to hook several moves over a string of bomber fixed heads; modern ratings can be like this. You'll find that ratings also take on their own character in different places on different rock types. A route rated A3 on flawless granite in California's Yosemite is very different from one rated A3 on the crumbling sandstone found in Utah's Fisher Towers.

Your first few wall climbs should be on routes that aren't too long, committing, or hard. For your first multiday wall experience, choose a climb that won't take you more than a week to complete and is within your climbing ability. My first wall was Zodiak on Yosemite's El Capitan; it took four petrifying days. At the end, I was so elated we were done, as well as totally worn out from the grip of fear, exposure, lack of sleep, dehydration, and all the hard work.

Do your research about the area and the route. Talk to other climbers who have done the route and ask at a local climbing shop about the latest information, conditions, and recommended rack.

Choosing a route that doesn't take too much time still teaches you a lot about planning for a larger climb. You will learn to judge the amount of time each pitch takes, what your pace is like, how much food and water to bring, what you forgot, whether you liked the exposure, and if you feel like stepping it up another notch without it being too much of an epic.

Build up your skills by incrementally bumping up the length and difficulty of routes. A short route might appear to be easy, but if it's sustained in difficulty, is overhanging, and has awkward pitches and a long descent, you might find that it is harder than a longer, more moderate route with straightforward climbing.

If your first few walls go well, giving you a boost of confidence, don't forget that things can get tangled into a big mess, and a hard pitch you thought wouldn't take too much time may take you hours to lead. If you drop a crucial piece of gear such as a jumar or a pulley, or if a storm pins you down for a day, your plans may be totally thrown off, leading to a frantic retreat or a drawn-out epic for the top. The more experience you gain taking one step at a time will ready you for the wall climb of your life.

With each new route, you'll gain greater knowledge of what you're capable of; use that to determine where you'll go next. Each skill takes time to learn and master. You don't master A5 hooking by starting on the Wyoming Sheep Ranch route on Yosemite's El Capitan. Just as in learning to climb the biggest routes in the world, you start on the smaller ones and work your way up.

Going big requires time and respect for the rock as well as skills developed through experience. Once you feel totally confident in your judgment, equipment skills, ability to climb long, sustained aid pitches, and knowledge of systems for getting up a big wall, then you can step it up a notch to the next level. However, after making the decision based on your experience, make sure that you're ready to lead anything that comes at you on your next route.

Doing one or two walls a year is a typical amount for an average climber. Every year the wall you climb might be taller, harder, and more demanding. With only a few walls a year, it might take you a few pitches of climbing to get back in the rhythm of wall climbing before you feel confident to take it a notch higher. Your experience will meter how hard you want to take it and what your threshold is; choosing the right route can make all the difference.

CHOOSING A PARTNER

Most wall-climbing teams include two people but can include three or more, depending on what you want to do: the smaller

Jared Ogden jumarring on the first ascent of Book of Shadows (VII 5.10 A3+ M6), on Trango Tower, Pakistan. Photo by Willy Benegas.

the group, the less gear and water you have to carry, whereas a larger team is more social and divides the labor more evenly.

If you're a budding wall climber, it's wise to climb with a more-experienced partner. Choosing a partner who has more experi-

ence than you is a benefit worth looking for because you'll learn a lot by watching instead of by making mistakes. You'll learn faster than if you climb with a less-experienced partner; ask a lot of questions along the way. The more-experienced climber can lead the more-demanding pitches, giving you the opportunity to see how it's done without much risk.

Going with a team of three, with the two other climbers having more experience than you, will help you gain invaluable lessons on your first wall. Not only will you learn more with experienced climbers, you'll be able to use their expensive equipment (such as portaledges and haul bags) without shelling out your life savings, and should you decide wall climbing is not for you, you will not have invested in unnecessary gear. Climbing in a team of three spreads out the workload, there's safety in numbers, and it creates a more social atmosphere. It requires more food and water to be hauled, but it is more efficient overall. I learned so much more about climbing as a team of three because I could talk through different strategies and systems as we climbed. A team of three can transform a novice climber into a good wall climber over the course of a single wall by showing and telling anything and everything there is to know on the route and giving hands-on experience while under supervision.

I learned a lot from my early partners who had more experience than I did, and it helped me through the panic attacks I had on the way. I admired their skill and the patience they had for me when I was fumbling around. Being patient may be the most important attribute a wall climber can have, and as you gain experience, remember that you might find yourself climbing with a less-experienced climber in the

future who deserves the same patience you received.

If you want to have a good experience wall climbing, choose a good partner. It doesn't matter how hard you climb. What matters most is how much fun you're having doing it. There will be partners you never climb with again and ones you'll always want to climb with. The experience with friends is what you remember in the end. You might remember a really hard lead, but you're going to remember who you were with more than the climbing. This kind of friendship can be hard to find but will make your climbing more successful.

Before you commit to any wall with a new partner, get to know that person by talking about climbing style, technique, safety, and how you both go about tasks while climbing. Talking with your partner about what your ambitions are, your climbing goals, the style in which you want to climb, and your attitude toward these is essential because it allows you and your partner to gel as a team long before you get on a wall. If you have a similar philosophy toward life and climbing, then you'll most likely make a solid team. If you're arguing about mundane things all the way to the base of the climb, you might be headed for a troubling climb.

My best partners have been people with whom I don't talk too much about climbing because we know exactly what each other's jobs are and how we're going to go about the game. This knowledge was gained through many climbing experiences that started with casual conversations in a campground or at the crags. If you're interested in trying to free climb the A1 but your partner just wants to aid everything and get up the route fast, talk these things over and find a middle ground where you both get what you want out of the climb. I've heard a lot of partners yelling at each other on a climb or during retreat because they had different expectations for a climb and just simply clashed on everything, which ultimately resulted in a failed climb.

If you're on a climb and you start having problems with your partner, put your ego aside and flush things out. Being honest is the best way to go. If you're afraid of something, be brave and let it out. Chances are, you just need some encouragement and support from your partner to ensure that you're on the same page. If you don't want to lead, your partner might, or vice versa. I remember a climb on Shipton Spire in Pakistan with Mark Synnott; I was frustrated at the weather and the commitment of the climbing. I boiled over and took it out on Mark. We talked right then about how we needed to support each other and I apologized for my attitude. We continued on to the summit and had one of the best climbs of our lives.

If you can't trust your partner, things will deteriorate. After all, you have your lives in one another's hands. If you're going to be critical about something, make it safety. Give positive reinforcement to your partner, especially for the hard jobs such as a difficult lead or haul. If things get ugly, say, while you're in the middle of a really miserable job such as hauling after a hard

pitch and it starts raining halfway through, crack a few tasteless jokes, make fun of yourself, and keep a healthy amount of sarcasm going; I've found this to make light of even the worst scenarios: "Yeah, I really do like sleeping in this wet bag on this cold, lumpy, sloping ledge three thousand feet off the ground."

PLANNING A CLIMB

OK, so now you have a route in mind and a solid partner, but you're not sure whether the route you want to do—say, the Wyoming Sheep Ranch (VI, 5.9, A5+) on Yosemite's El Capitan—is the right choice. To go about deciding which route would suit both your ability levels, be honest with yourself and your partner from the start. If you've never done a wall but have done a considerable amount of climbing over the years, you can feel confident in your basic climbing skills, backed by your experience.

Base your decision on both your and your partner's skills. If you want to climb a hard route but aren't sure you want to lead the crux, see if your partner has the ability and willingness to do it. This is an excellent way to watch and learn how harder pitches are put together. If you're a solid 5.10 free climber and your partner is a solid A3 climber but not so good at free climbing, then pool your skills and sort out who gets the crux pitches in his or her strengths. If neither of you have much experience in aid climbing, you can practice by aiding a free climb (without using pitons) locally that will get you somewhat prepared for a bigger climb of easy difficulty, such as Zion National Park's Touchstone Wall (III, 5.9, C2).

After you've chosen your route and partner, your next step is planning the time when you will do the climb. For a successful trip, also consider the length of the climb, its difficulty, the possibility of weather delays, and the altitude.

Assess the duration of the climb. If you plan on climbing a route that has sustained difficulty with technical aspects of the climbing—combined with fear—that can slow you down, plan on three or four pitches a day. Sometimes you might get in only one or two. For example, leading one of the headwall pitches on the Shield on Yosemite's El Capitan might take a novice or intermediate climber 2–4 hours to complete. On the other hand, if there are a lot of moderate pitches and only a few harder ones, you might get in four to seven pitches a day, especially if you do some free climbing. Factor in that you could take a fall and have to relead a hard section. This will take more time than you planned on.

Altitude, not much of a factor with most wall climbing destinations in the United States, can severely alter your ability to perform anything, much less climbing. Coming down with Acute Mountain Sickness (AMS) or pulmonary or cerebral edema can kill you. There have been cases of all of these at relatively low elevations, so don't be fooled into thinking you can't get it at a lower elevation. Staying hydrated and acclimatizing are the best ways to allow your body to adjust to higher altitude. The rule of thumb is to climb high and sleep low.

If you're going to the Diamond on Longs Peak in Colorado's Rocky Mountain National Park, you'll probably bivy at the base of the wall the night before and start climbing the next morning. There's a high probability that a climber could get altitude sickness in this situation. If you feel lightheaded or have altitude symptoms (read *Medicine for Mountaineering* by James A. Wilkerson), don't start climbing. Descend and allow your body to adjust at a slower pace. I've had painful headaches from climbing too high too fast and was forced to descend, which delayed the climb. Once I adjusted properly, I was fine.

Other than altitude sickness, the thinner air at high altitudes takes its toll on your muscles, lungs, and blood. Because you'll have to breath harder to get more oxygen into your system, your throat will dry out faster than it would normally and you might find yourself getting tired faster. Drop your climbing ability by a solid number grade the first time you climb at a higher altitude to see how you can handle the altitude. You'll find a 5.10 is much harder at 14,000 feet than a solid 5.11 is at 2000 feet. The only way to increase your ability at altitude is by adjusting properly to the altitude and then climbing up there. Train all you can before the climb, but no matter what, you'll need time to adjust to thinner air.

A higher-altitude environment has colder temperatures and a greater possibility of storms, so being prepared for harsh weather is a greater concern. If you plan on climbing a wall in winter, be prepared for

freezing temperatures, snowstorms, and short days. For these kinds of outings, bring warmer clothing and more food, since you burn more calories just to stay warm.

Make a list of what you need and go over it so many times you memorize it. The obvious items on the list include all the climbing gear, ropes, and hardware for a multiday route. Check off each item as you pack it into a haul bag. Before leaving for a big climb, I'll call my partner three or four times to talk about details, making sure I don't miss a thing.

Let family or friends know when and where you're going to be climbing and your intended time of return. Some national parks and monuments with big walls, such as the Black Canyon of the Gunnison and Zion, require climbers to check in and out with the rangers. This lets people know whether you're late returning from your climb and helps facilitate a rescue, if necessary (self-rescue is covered in Chapter 4).

STYLE AND ETHICS

In the pursuit of climbing, you have to be honest, with yourself and others. As with anything in life that demands honesty, climbing has always involved decisions about style and ethics, which are found at its roots. Types of climbing currently include alpine climbing, wall climbing, sport and traditional climbing, ice and mixed climbing, bouldering, mountaineering, and competition climbing.

Because there are many styles and ethics to believe in, there will always be controversy about them. However, style and ethics are learned through experience: knowing what other styles and ethics there are and adapting them to create your own, you develop a sense of what you believe is right. When you've got your own set of style and ethics, you can start putting them to use, whether it's on speed ascents, free ascents, or first ascents. By each climber striving for the highest standards possible, the climbing community will remain healthy.

CLIMBING STYLES

Attitudes toward aid-climbing and free-climbing ascents have changed dramatically through the actions of bold, talented climbers who've led the different aspects of big wall climbing into the future. These actions always improved on style and efficiency, with technology playing a crucial role in the advancement of the sport.

When the Nose on Yosemite's El Capitan was first climbed in 1958, it was an unbelievable achievement in big wall aid climbing that required months to achieve. With the introduction of new gear in the 1960s and 1970s, the limits of aid climbing skyrocketed.

Then in 1978, the Nose got its first one-day ascent, influencing the perception of

Russel Mitchrovitch on a speed ascent of the Jet Stream, (VI 5.11 A4), Half Dome, Yosemite National Park

what was possible by using a mix of free and aid climbing to set the speed record.

In 1992 Lynn Hill freed the Nose in three days, another unbelievable accomplishment, and then returned a year later to improve on her own style by freeing the route in one day! In 2002, after several teams had shaved the record time down to hours and minutes, Hans Florine and Yuji Hirayama speed climbed the Nose in an unbelievable 2 hours, 48 minutes, and 55 seconds!

Today new ideas are born, speed ascent records are being broken, technology is advancing, and the pool of talented climbers is growing, while at the same time, today's climbers are maintaining the highest ethical standards.

When Todd Skinner and Paul Piana completed the first free ascent of the Salathe Wall in Yosemite in 1988, it was a catalyst for future big wall routes to go free. Since then, the number of big wall aid routes going free has exploded. Examples of the talent, vision, and determination to further the sport of big wall climbing include ascents of routes such as the Regular and Direct Northwest Face routes on Yosemite's Half Dome; the south face of Mount Watkins in Yosemite; El Niño, El Corazon, the Golden Gate, Freerider, the Muir Wall, the west face, the west buttress, the Dihedral Wall, and the Nose on El Capitan; and the Hallucinogen Wall in Colorado's Black Canyon of the Gunnison.

In the greater ranges of the world, climbers have applied these styles on some of the biggest walls on the planet. Shipton Spire and the Trango Towers area, both in Pakistan, have seen a wealth of new routes, both free and aid, in the past eight years.

In the Patagonia region of Argentina and Chile, climbers have been pushing standards for more than 30 years. The area's constant stormy weather—combined with dangerous approaches; long, steep granite towers; and challenging climbing—makes any ascent there especially rewarding. The biggest gem is Fitzroy: one of the longest rock faces in the world, offering unlimited possibilities on a beautiful yet ethereal mountain. The 2001–02 season was markedly successful, with more climbable days than anyone can remember, culminating in a slew of cutting-edge new routes and unheard-of speed ascents. The season was highlighted by Dean Potter's solo ascents on Cerro Torre and Fitzroy.

Speed climbing has turned into a race against the clock. Unfortunately, it has also turned into a race between climbers for the fastest time on a route. When grade VI routes were being done in less than 24 hours, it cut the time down by days. Now times are being cut by only minutes.

Free climbing and speed climbing existing aid routes are current trends in big wall climbing, followed closely by insanely hard solo aid routes and free solos. The enchainment of multiple big wall routes inspired by Peter Croft and John Bacher was used by Dean Potter and Tim O'Neil to

Topher Donahue scouting, Black Canyon of the Gunnison National Park

link up El Capitan, Half Dome, and Mount Watkins in a single day, an achievement that will inspire generations of climbers to come. In 2000 Peter Croft and Conrad Anker climbed an 8000-foot-long 5.11 free climb in Pakistan. In Colorado's Black Canyon of the Gunnison, Mike Pennings and Jeff Hollenbaugh linked up the South and North Chasm View Walls with the Painted Wall in a day for an outstanding feat of endurance and vision.

ETHICS

It's imperative that you not add bolts to an existing route. You have to respect the first ascent and the style in which it was climbed. If a bolt is broken or has fallen out, then replace it with a new one. If you come up to an old anchor with question-able bolts and there's nothing else to integrate into the anchor, remove one of the old bolts by hammering a series of thin to thick pitons behind the hanger to force it out. Then drill a $3/8$-inch-diameter hole $2^{1}/_{4}$ inches deep and place a new stainless-steel five-piece bolt. Don't just add another -inch or $5/_{16}$-inch bolt to an already bogus anchor. I've seen this too often and what happens is ugly, multiple new small bolts. Instead, use multiple pieces of gear all equalized.

Many British climbers have refused to use bolts at all and believe that it's better to leave a route in its natural state than to bolt it, because someday someone will be able to climb it without bolts. This dogma, referred to as "head-pointing," has led to insane routes such as Equilibrium (E10 7c, E signifying Extremely Severe), a single pitch of 5.14 climbing with basi-cally no protection; a fall would spell your end.

Head-pointing involves, but is not limited to, top-rope rehearsal to the point where you feel you can lead the route without falling, or at least you hope so. A lot of the classic head-point routes are single-pitch routes on which any fall would have you closing in on ground zero, which makes for higher stakes. Applying these ethics to wall climbing contributes to the highest standards of commitment and ensures that those who don't have the ability to do such a route have something to aspire to.

Two recent big wall "head-point"-style ascents worth mention include La Bella Vista route on the Cima Grande in the Italian Dolomites, free climbed by Alex Huber at 5.14b on the original and/or existing pitons and natural gear, and Mauro "Bubu" Bole's free ascent of the Cime Ouest, also in the Italian Dolomites, at 5.13d, also on all natural gear. These are considered a few of the top contenders in rock climbing big walls with high-end difficulty, matched with intense commitment.

Chipping holds, enhancing the rock's natural features, and dishonest reporting are all unacceptable behavior. Chipping holds on all natural free or aid routes is just not ethical, fair, or honest. Don't do it, period. The same goes for enhancing hook placements or copper-head placements or any other way in which you purposely alter the rock.

Our climbing resources need your attention. Climbing has become more commercialized and affluent in the world community than ever before. We're faced with more trash, environmental impacts, and growing numbers of users on the same resources without properly planning for such problems. As climbers, we try to police ourselves, but we have to give more attention to conservation and protection than we have in the past. By contributing time and money to groups such as the Access Fund and the American Alpine Club (see Appendix A, Climbing Resources), we'll maintain our resources for future generations to enjoy.

THE FUTURE OF WALL CLIMBING

The climbers of today are setting new standards and creating new styles and techniques that will become the code for the future. The best climbers of the world are applying their skills to the big routes and walls, eliminating the aid climbing and creating amazingly difficult free climbs or pushing the limits of aid climbing. Climbers such as the Huber brothers, Yuji Hiriyama, Tommy and Beth Caldwell, and Lynn Hill have set the pace for free climbing on El Capitan and elsewhere. With 5.13 free climbs on the high-altitude walls in Pakistan, 5.14 free climbs on El Capitan, and 5.14 runout free climbs in Europe, the future of wall climbing is limited by only our minds.

CHAPTER 2

Dan Steves on Astrodog (V 5.11+), Black Canyon of the Gunnison National Park

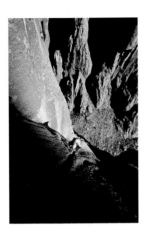

Basic Wall-Climbing Procedures

The typical wall-climbing scenario involves two climbers rotating leads, which involves the leader leading a pitch while belayed from below, reaching the next anchor position and building a new belay anchor, then belaying up the second while hauling the bag after the lead. The second, meanwhile, follows and cleans the pitches, then prepares to lead the next pitch. The pair might climb as many as several pitches a day. If it's a one-day climb, they will walk off from the top, descend the wall, or perhaps retreat before reaching the top. They may have to bivy and continue the next day in the same fashion, but for multiday wall climbs, see Chapter 3, Advanced Techniques.

Multipitch climbing is very demanding and requires a high level of skill to perform. Managing all the gear while trying to complete a route in a day or just trying to get to the next bivy can fry your nerves and create an unbearable amount of stress. This stress can be magnified by your interaction with your climbing partner, the surroundings, and, of course, the threat of weather.

GETTING STARTED

When you're in the middle of climbing a pitch, your sole focus is how you'll climb the next section of rock, place or remove the next piece of gear, make a move that requires a burst of energy, then find a chance to recover and move on. There isn't much else going on but your connection to the rock and the environment that surrounds you. All the tensions of life fall away, leaving you with the task of climbing. It's that simple.

There are, however, things that can cause this serenity to be disrupted. By understanding fall factors and impact forces, doing proper research on the chosen route and bringing a climbers topo, and preparing your gear correctly, you can avoid glitches in the system and have a better time climbing.

UNDERSTANDING FALL FACTOR AND IMPACT FORCE

Each type of climbing rope is given a standards test by the Union Internationale des Associations d'Alpinisme (UIAA) to determine the number of falls it will hold before failure, its elongation, and its impact force. The UIAA then assigns a series of numbers to the rope showing this information. This information is useful for understanding and comparing rope characteristics.

The UIAA performs a static drop test in a controlled tower that is the same for any rope. It measures how many standard falls the rope can take. The standard test creates a 1.75 fall factor (see next page), on a scale that goes to only 2. A weight of 80 kg (for single and twin ropes) or 55 kg (for half ropes) falls on a single cord (single and half ropes) or a doubled cord (twin ropes). The weight is dropped $16\frac{1}{2}$ feet on $8\frac{1}{4}$ feet of rope over an edge similar to a carabiner's. Between each fall test, there is almost no delay, which would allow the rope to recover, and the weight falls on the same spot in each fall test. This heightens the impact force on each drop by removing more elongation from the rope and ultimately exceeds the rope's tensile strength, so it breaks. Single and half ropes have to withstand at least five standard falls; a doubled twin rope, at least 12 standard falls.

This fall test can't be re-created in a real-world climbing situation. In addition, during these fall tests there is no friction created by a belay device, no force absorbed by knots tightening or a belayer being lifted, nor any force absorbed by the belayer paying out rope at the apex of the fall. All these factors apply in a real climbing situation, which reduces the amount of force created on the rope.

If you buy a type of rope that is given a falls-held number of 10, it doesn't mean that you have to retire it after 10 leader falls. Dynamic ropes can withstand hundreds of falls and are retired when they are no longer safe: when their elongation has diminished and the sheath has deteriorated. A rope won't break in normal climbing conditions, providing the rope is safe from being cut on a sharp edge.

The working elongation of a rope represents its elasticity under a static load. The UIAA also performs a dynamic elongation test in which the rope is preloaded with a 5-kg weight, then loaded with 80 kg: elongation cannot exceed 10 percent for single and twin ropes and 12 percent for half ropes. Ropes are then given a first-fall elongation number. The UIAA maximum permissible is 40 percent. This dynamic elongation test represents the inertial properties of a rope better than the static test does. A higher elongation creates more force on protection. You want a rope with 25 percent to 35 percent dynamic elongation. This is helpful to determine whether a rope will stretch a lot during hauling or top-roping.

Fall factor. A fall factor is the relative measurement of force created in a fall. It is calculated by dividing the length of rope in the system by the length of the fall: a 10-foot fall on 10 feet of rope creates a factor 1 fall. A 20-foot fall on 10 feet of rope creates a factor 2 fall. This happens when a climber falls from 10 feet above the belay; it is the worst kind of fall you can take. If you climb 100 feet and fall 10 feet over your last protection, you'll fall 20 feet but create only a factor 0.2 fall (20 divided by 100). A climber placing consistently solid protection, especially right off the belay, will protect him- or herself and prevent the system from creating a high fall factor.

Impact force. The impact force is the measurement for the hardness of a fall. It is the maximum force created by a falling climber that affects the load in a fall. When the fall is over, the impact force is absorbed by the rope's elongation and, ultimately, by the falling climber. Ropes with a higher impact force number create a harder fall on the climber and more force on the system. Ropes with a lower impact force number create a softer but longer fall on the climber and put lower force on the system. The maximum impact force allowed by the UIAA is 2680 pounds. Most ropes have a breaking strength of around 5000 pounds.

The impact force number given to a rope is shown in measurements of force called kilonewtons (kN). One kilonewton is approximately equal to the force of 220 pounds. A typical single-rated 10.5 mm rope will have an impact force of approximately 9 kN, or 1980 pounds. A typical double-rated 8.5–9 mm set of ropes will have an impact force of around 5 kN, or 1100 pounds. You can see that the difference in diameter and the use of double ropes create considerable differences in impact forces. For most walls, you'll want a single-rated rope of 9.5–11 mm diameter with a low impact force number. Double ropes aren't suited well for the duties of wall climbing.

ROUTEFINDING

Successful routefinding begins with gathering as much information about a climb as possible from guidebooks, maps, illustrations, photos, and, most important, someone who's already done the route. Route descriptions from guidebooks can be useful as a general guide, but they generally don't convey the exposure, difficulties, or amount of skill required of the climbing team. Studying all the information gathered will give you a solid foundation about the route, what crack system it follows on the wall, and what features it includes. Even with this information, it can be difficult to tell which way to go, what crack to follow, or whether the route goes out over a roof or traverses off to the side.

Use a climbers topo, a map written by the first ascensionist describing in detail exactly where the route goes. It is written just to keep us on route. Also bring a picture of the climb to help keep you on track. The problem with topos is that they can be vague, misleading, and hard to read. Although they do provide additional information about the route, one of the best ways to read a route is to look at the wall itself.

Using your naked eye, a pair of binoculars, or a spotting scope allows you to scout the climb from a distance. Locate features that may be useful for ascent, and make a mental note of them. Such features include weaknesses in the cliff; crack systems that are continuous and ones that aren't; blank headwalls and alternative routes around them; roofs that may be impassable; and dihedrals, chimneys, and trees or bushes indicating a belay ledge. Remember that once you're below the climb itself, you might not be able to see the whole route.

RACKING YOUR EQUIPMENT

Because wall climbing usually requires you to bring hordes of gear, you need to rack and organize it in a way that makes it easy to access and keeps it from turning into a total cluster. You'll have an assortment of pins, stoppers, camming units, hooks, heads, slings, quickdraws, nonlocking carabiners, a pulley, the ropes, and all your other gear. Always rack your gear the same way so it's always in the same order.

The first place to start racking is your chest harness. A lot of your gear should be kept on the chest harness while you're aid

---

KEY EXERCISE: ROUTEFINDING

Stand at the base of a route with a photo and topo of it. Study the topo and photo, and compare them to the route itself to determine where you would belay and where the route goes, creating a mental map of the route. Once you're on the climb, refer back to your mental map. Practice this as often as you can, even if you don't actually climb the route.

climbing. This distributes the weight evenly on your shoulders and keeps it easily accessible. It also keeps extra weight off your main harness, which already has a lead line and a tag line attached to it, and keeps it from grinding into your waist. Most chest harnesses have at least one, if not two, gear loops on each side.

On one side put your camming units, each racked with its own biner, from smallest to largest, front to back. This way

you always know that the small cams are near the front and the larger ones in the back for easy access.

On the other side, rack your stoppers on one biner, with one full set and RPs or small stoppers also on one biner, though usually you can fit two sets on one biner. I put the small stoppers closer to the front as I do with the cams. Rack your pins, hooks, and copper heads, if you're using them, on this side as well. I like to put no more than

Cams racked on the chest harness from small to big, front to back, and quickdraws clipped to the front gear loops on the harness

Spare biners, pitons, micropitons, nuts, and knifeblades racked on the chest harness, cordelette and quickdraws clipped to the harness

four pins on an oval biner because they rack better: any more and it's hard to manage them. Decide whether you want to place all the same kind of pins on a biner or an assortment. I prefer to put, say, four different-size knifeblades on one, four small to medium angles on another, and so on. This way I pull off the blades and I have four sizes to choose from instead of four totally different pins for different sizes.

Rack your hooks on this side on an oval biner, with two to three different hooks per biner, for a total of about six assorted hooks. If you have copper heads, put five to eight assorted sizes per biner on the same side as the pins. If there is room on this side, include three to four free biners clipped together in a string.

Rack everything else on your main harness. Start by clipping the haul line in to

---

KEY EXERCISE: PRACTICE RACKING

Set up a racking system that works for you, then practice racking until you've got it wired. Use a checklist such as this:

CHEST HARNESS, LEFT SIDE
- camming units: smallest in front, largest in back

CHEST HARNESS, RIGHT SIDE
- stoppers: two full sets on two biners, smallest in front
- pins: four blades on one oval biner, four angles on one oval biner, etc.
- hooks: six—two or three different ones per oval biner
- copper heads: five to eight per biner
- free biners: three to four clipped together in a string

MAIN HARNESS, FULL-STRENGTH BACK LOOP
- haul line: clip in with a locking biner and a pulley prerigged to haul
- jumars: clip in a pair with a locking biner

MAIN HARNESS, REAR GEAR LOOPS
- cordelette: clip in for use in the anchor
- hammer: girth-hitch it

MAIN HARNESS, FRONT GEAR LOOPS
- quickdraws: clip to both sides for quick access
- tie-offs: clip 10 on a single biner

the full-strength loop on the back of your harness with a locking biner and the pulley, prerigged to haul; clip a pair of jumars in to this same place with another locking biner. For your hammer, you can use a hammer holster that slides over your waist belt or an over-the-shoulder sling with the hammer girth-hitched to it, or you can girth-hitch it to one of your rear gear loops or your chest harness with enough length to swing the hammer over your head. If you choose the latter, you can either use a biner and clip it in to a gear loop or holster it in one of the gear loops on your harness. Rack your quickdraws, if you use them, on both sides of the front gear loop for quick access. If you have tie-offs, you can rack up to 10 on a single biner and clip them to your harness because they don't weigh much. You can carry shoulder slings over your chest harness and clip a cordelette for use in the anchor on the rear loop.

LEADING

Leading is the most exciting and rewarding part of climbing. There are, however, many things that can disrupt this happy state. Leading a pitch that's more difficult than you're able to climb, not having the right kind of gear or the right amount of it, or having to do a pendulum or tension traverse without knowing about it in advance can stress you out. When you're leading, you need to be aware of these things and keep good track of how much gear you have left on your rack.

ROUTEFINDING ON LEAD

Before setting off on a pitch, use your eyes to scout out potential features, cracks, and holds and where the route looks as though it would go. Keep an eye out for alternate lines, holds, and resting spots too. Even after you have a mental map of the pitch, continue scouting out the climbing ahead as you go, making changes to the original plan if features and holds turn out not to be as feasible as they looked from a distance or if you find holds that you previously didn't notice.

Be prepared to look around the corner for alternatives that were previously out of sight: these may be easier than what lies directly ahead. Keep in mind that some pitches require a tension traverse or a pendulum to gain the next crack system or dihedral and that the next crack system might not be visible from where you are. Throughout the climb, make note of possible retreats in case you can't continue and possible descent routes if there isn't one indicated or established.

Here's an example of how to stay on route. Let's say you're leading a pitch that climbs up moderate face terrain, but you can't find any fixed gear or a bolt to assure you that you're on the right route. After consulting the topo, choose a direction that looks as though it might be right and climb until it either goes or doesn't go, keeping in mind that if it doesn't, you'll have to down-climb to where you started. You might sometimes see a fixed nut or pin with some slings on it indicating a bail-off point, a pendulum point, or a rappel anchor. They often lead climbers astray from the route, but they might be worth investigating if other possibilities don't work out. Explore the other possibilities until you find the right way, consulting the topo and the information you gathered from the base.

If you don't find any way that works, you might have climbed a pitch or more higher than the way you were supposed to go. Consider every option before you rappel. If you have to rappel, you should be able to find where you got off route and continue on in the right direction. Above all else, trust your intuition and judgment to find your way up or retreat.

RACKING FOR THE LEAD

If you can get your partner to rack the gear the same way you do, then you both will know where everything is on the chest harness. This is also helpful when your partner cleans a pitch, because the gear will be reracked in the same place and ready to go on the next pitch.

I always bring a cleaning tool on lead for digging out dirt, setting stoppers in funky cracks, or extracting a stuck cam I've misplaced. The remainder of items, such as a belay-rappel device and locking biner, optional belay gloves, and a water bottle, can be distributed where they are out of the way (on your waist belt's rear gear loops, for example) because you won't be needing them while leading. Use the system that works for you: each climber has his or her own style of racking.

Clip the tag line to the back of your waist-belt harness so the rope is out of the way but easy to reach and remove when needed. I always set up the tag line through the haul pulley so it's ready when I reach the next belay. I clip it to my harness with a locking biner so I can't lose it and so I have a locking biner for the pulley at the belay. Stack the tag line at the belay so a loop doesn't snag below, and place it where the belayer can access it quickly.

Resupplying. When leading a wall climb, some strategy in racking is useful. Let's say you're about to start leading a long A3 pitch and it looks as though it's mostly going to use thin pins, cams, and stoppers, but you can't see around a roof about halfway up the pitch or how big the crack is. Start leading with some free biners, quickdraws, slings, an assortment of small cams, small stoppers, and a good selection of maybe eight pins, but leave the rest of the gear behind.

If you need more gear during a pitch, use the tag line to pull it up. The belayer clips the gear to the rope, using a clove hitch because it doesn't require you to untie any knots. Overhand, figure eight, and butterfly knots can also be used. The belayer clips in one piece of gear to the clove hitch and clips the rest of the gear to that biner so you can easily remove and rack the gear. Once all the gear is removed, you drop the rope back to the belayer.

This eliminates the need to carry all the gear from the start of the pitch. In the example above, once you've made it to the roof and can see that the crack gets bigger and that you'll need large cams, have your belayer clip the larger cams and additional free biners and quickdraws to your haul line for you to pull up, and then continue climbing. Remember, call for more gear no later than halfway up the length of your lead rope; otherwise, the tag line won't reach you.

The belayer should never let go of the end of the tag line. If you're more than halfway up, your belayer can extend the tag line with another rope in order for the extra gear to reach you. It's common to extend it with the remainder of the lead rope or with a third rope, if you brought one. If you don't have rope to extend the tag line, you can always get lowered off a good piece of gear to a point where you can get the gear, and while you're lowered you can also take out some of the gear you have already placed on the pitch so you can reuse it higher up.

The nice thing about this "resupply" method is that you're not burdened with all the heavy rack from the start and can carry only what you'll need. If you find you don't need a rack of pins or other gear, you can always clip it on to your haul line and zip it back to the belay. Leading with a light rack is advantageous when you anticipate some free climbing or climbing up a chimney, where excessive gear restricts movement, or when you plan on doing a section of hooking.

Leapfrogging placements. A common practice to eliminate carrying too much gear is to leapfrog camming devices while climbing easier sections of a pitch. This means removing the previous piece each time you place a new one. If you encounter a section of the pitch that is a similar size

for more than 20 feet, you can use two of the same pieces of gear in this way instead of leaving a piece of gear every 4 feet and having to carry extra pieces. Once you reach a section where the size changes, you can leave one piece for protection and keep the other one for farther up. This is faster and lighter for both the leader and follower. With some practice, you'll be more efficient and have a great time.

ROUTING THE ROPE

When you're leading, skillful rope routing protects your rope and reduces friction on the system. Always try to keep your rope from running over sharp or rough edges, through cracks, or behind rocks to keep it from getting stuck or worn or, in the case of a fall, breaking. Also try to place protection where it will keep your rope away from loose blocks and water. Use long runners, which allow the rope to hang away from the rock, reducing rope drag and keeping the rope from shifting a piece of gear.

Remember that your partner will be jumarring the rope while cleaning the pitch. This takes out a fair amount of the rope's elongation and causes it to become taut. When the rope is taut, it cuts on edges faster and is more susceptible to abrasion. Make sure you route the rope properly for safety.

DOING TENSION TRAVERSES AND PENDULUMS

Tension traverses and pendulums offer two ways of reaching other features such as ledges and cracks that are otherwise accessible only by drilling a bolt ladder to them. When doing traversing pitches or pendulums, make sure you have a way to backtrack if retreat becomes necessary.

Tension traverses. These are used more on short distances and on lower-angled faces. The climber leans away from the rope, using it for balance, and, using his or her feet, climbs across a section using friction and available holds. The belayer slowly pays out rope while maintaining tension without jerking the climber backward or paying out too much slack, causing the climber to lose control. Communication between the climber and belayer is as follows:

Climber: "Tension."

Belayer: "OK. You have tension."

Climber: "OK. Slowly lower me out as I move across."

When the climber reaches the chosen place where tension is no longer needed, he or she lets the belayer know.

Climber: "OK. I don't need tension anymore. I'm climbing again."

Belayer: "OK. I'm watching you."

The second climber will typically need tension to follow unless he or she is on jumars. To follow, repeat the same steps as above.

Pendulums. To pendulum, the climber places a solid piece of protection above the area to be crossed, clips the rope in, and is lowered to a point where the swing can begin. The belayer holds the climber here and doesn't let out any slack. At this point, the climber runs back and forth while hanging from the rope till the ledge, crack,

or feature can be reached. The climber uses one hand to hold onto the rope and uses the other for balance while running back and forth. If the height isn't right, the climber can be lowered down or climb back up for a better position. Maintaining communication with the belayer is critical for precise pendulums. Be careful not to rub the rope against sharp edges during the swing, especially if multiple swings are necessary, because it can cause rope damage.

Sometimes a pendulum can be completed by using a series of handholds in conjunction with a tension traverse. The King Swing on the Nose route on Yosemite's El Capitan is a good example. Once the climber is running back and forth with enough speed, he or she uses the momentum to swing to the apex of the pendulum, where the climber must grab a featured arête with the hands. From here, the climber uses tension, available handholds, and friction with the feet to climb into a good crack in a corner that isn't visible from the bottom of the pendulum point.

Once the leader has completed a pendulum and must continue climbing higher, he or she should climb as high as safely possible before placing more protection, to reduce rope drag and to protect the second from a long fall when he or she follows the pendulum. If the belay is made under the pendulum point, the second climbs only as high as the leader to the pendulum point and repeats the swing. If there is gear to clean leading up to the pendulum point, then the second cleans it, lowers off the point, and then follows the swing.

Keep an eye out for where you're going when swinging on a pendulum.

Hold onto the rope with one hand while extending the other for the hold.

The piece of gear used for the pendulum point isn't retrievable. The second climber will have to use the same piece to follow the pendulum, whether free climbing or jumarring. It's best to use two pieces unless one is a solid piece of gear or a bolt because a fall while swinging could lead to serious injury.

If you must retreat past a pendulum, it is usually possible if you climb one to two pitches beyond the pendulum point and swing back to the original line on rappel, clipping in to the point on the way or placing gear to keep you on track to the next rappel station. The second on rappel removes the gear.

FALLING

Obviously, falling is part of the climbing game. It will happen to all of us at some point, especially when we're pushing our

Once you've grabbed the hold, use both hands and start free climbing or aiding.

limits. It's as much a mind game as a physical game "on the sharp end of the rope" (in other words, when you're leading), so the more accustomed to falling you are, the more confident you'll be.

On big walls, try to minimize the length and frequency of falls because they're dangerous and will stress the rope and the belay system. There are many instances on a big wall when a fall can occur. Knowing how a fall affects the rope, the belay system, and yourself, and understanding the forces involved, will give you a clear understanding of the risks involved. To minimize the risk of falling, you can prepare for several things. Here is a review:

- Practice taking falls at the crag; then a fall while you're leading won't seem so dangerous because you're more relaxed and know how to fall correctly.
- Always wear a helmet while leading and belaying.
- Keep the rope running smooth and directed away from loose blocks, cracks, and sharp edges.
- Keep your belayer informed and on the

KEY EXERCISE: LEARNING TO FALL

Falling is never intuitive and always feels sketchy. Practice taking falls on purpose at a steep sport crag where a fall is nothing but air and a soft catch. This will make you trust the rope, your partner, and the belay system. Like a cat held over a pool of water, you'll learn how to fall with your legs down, poised and ready for action. With practice, you'll find that falling will become intuitive and won't seem terrifying, which will allow you to relax. Once you're relaxed, you start to climb more fluidly and strongly.

watch for potential falls or sketchy sections.

- Assess every placement for whether it would hold a fall.
- If you're too afraid to lead a section, consider letting your partner give it a go because down-aiding, especially on hooks, is difficult.
- Keep your feet and legs clear of getting tangled in the aiders and the lead line.
- Pay close attention when leading over ledges and on traverses, because a fall onto a ledge or swinging into a corner can cause serious injury.
- Let your partner know when you're getting near the end of the pitch so he or she can start preparing for the haul and cleaning the pitch.

If you do take a fall, allow your rope to recover by clipping in directly to a solid piece of unweighted gear. This allows the fibers in the rope to rejuvenate from the stretch, bringing it back to its full potential.

BELAYING

Belaying is the single most critical element of safe climbing practice. You have to know how to belay in order to use a rope safely while climbing. The basic principle of a belay is that the person who is belaying holds the rope of the climber and, in case of a fall, stops the fall to reduce chances of injury to the climber. In big wall climbing, first the follower belays the leader from below to a higher belay point, then the leader belays the follower from above as the follower cleans the pitch. If the follower is going to jumar the rope to clean the pitch, the leader simply fixes the rope to the higher anchor and does not belay.

BELAY TECHNIQUES AND DEVICES

Belay techniques have evolved from simple hip belays to autolocking belay devices that have changed the way we look at belaying. A belay device works by creating a bend in the rope, which allows the belayer to feed out or take in rope; yet the use of a brake hand creates enough friction between the rope and the device to cause the rope to stop a fall. You can also belay with a Münter hitch clipped in to a locking carabiner; however, it can spin the ropes into a tangled mess if done improperly.

Belay devices. Several types of belay devices are available, including stitch plates, tubes, figure eights, and autolock devices such as the Petzl GriGri or the Trango Cinch. The most popular are the plate types and autolocking types. Consult the manufacturer's instructions on how to use any belay device. Any belay technique takes practice to learn properly. With all belay devices, you *never* take your brake hand off the rope! If you don't know how to set up a belay device or are unsure about the different types, seek professional instruction before attempting a big wall.

With the plate and tube devices, you make a bight in the rope, feed it through an opening in the device, and clip it in to a locking carabiner attached to your harness. A figure eight works in the same manner,

Various belay devices

although it isn't as functional and creates different amounts of friction, depending on how you set it up. The advantage of using a plate or tube device is that it gives a softer catch if a fall occurs, ultimately lowering the impact force on the climber and the gear. This is advantageous when the climber is leading on dubious placements that can pop out under extra stress, such as results from a fall onto an autolocking belay device.

Autolocking belay devices such as the GriGri need special instruction to operate, but generally they work by the rope pulling on a camming device inside that locks down on the rope and keeps it from sliding through. This type of device is used only for single-rope belaying and rappelling.

Single rope versus twin or double ropes. On most big walls, climbers tend to use a single rope as their main lead rope instead of twin or double ropes. The advantages of using a single rope are simplified handling and following on jumars; in addition, a single rope means less clutter at the tie-in point on your harness. When using a single rope, any of the belay devices mentioned above will suffice. Using a GriGri has become popular on walls because it allows the belayer more time to sort through gear, read, or stare off into the wilderness since the device will lock in the event of a fall. Remember, though, that ropes less than 10 mm in diameter do not work in a GriGri and you must *always* keep your brake hand on the rope even though you're using what is considered an autolocking belay device.

Belaying with two ropes means more rope management and can be very cumbersome for the belayer, but note that two ropes provide the highest safety margin. Twin or double ropes are used more often in an alpine environment, where you want the highest safety margin due to loose or sharp rock and have the option of rappelling the length of the ropes. If you use two ropes, you must use a stitch or tube device because a GriGri can be used only on a single rope. Using two ropes takes some practice, because each rope is clipped by itself, requiring the belayer to feed out and take in rope constantly, all the while maintaining a tangle-free pile of ropes.

When I was climbing Great Trango Tower in Pakistan in 1999, I noticed a unique belay system used by a group of Russian climbers. They would lead with two 10 mm ropes, clipping one rope 75 percent of the time and the other just occasionally. At the end of the lead, the rope that was clipped in to most of the gear was fixed for the second to jumar on for cleaning. The second rope, which the second climber tied in to, was used for belaying as if they were free climbing. This creates a foolproof safety system: if the rope the second is jumarring on is cut on an edge, the second is backed up by the second rope used to belay from above. Though it is perhaps redundant and cumbersome, this system is an alternative way to protect both the leader and follower from a rope-cutting fall.

BELAY POSITIONS AND ANCHORS

Entire books have been written on the subject of belay anchors, and if you don't already know the basics about building and using them, buy one of these books and learn how to build safe, bombproof anchors. This book discusses this topic only briefly, and as it relates specifically to big wall climbing.

Belay positions. On a wall climb, the belay is the most important link in the safety chain. Often a delicate lead is possible to do only if a safe, solid anchor can be made to protect the leader. Finding belay positions with good anchor placements and stances is a very important part of routefinding that is integral to the climbing system. While leading, keep your eyes open for good belay points. Established big wall routes usually have designated belay points, which makes it easy to locate the belay.

Solid anchors and stances are not the only considerations in selecting a belay position. The belayer, not having much room to move around, is vulnerable to falling objects. On any multipitch route, the belay should be, if possible, in a safe, sheltered place that's out of the fall line of the leader as well as anything that could fall from above. A small roof, a ledge, a stance around a corner, or an overhang all provide excellent places to make a belay for maximum protection. If you have the option of climbing a bit farther or cutting a pitch a little short to obtain a better belay position, it's worth it.

Anchors. Once you've decided where you're going to place your anchor, place at least three bomber A1 placements, preferably above a ledge or under a roof. If you can't get three A1 placements, add more pieces of gear. Big wall anchors should always be multidirectional, must be able to hold a minimum of 2000 pounds, and must be able to hold long falls without failure. If you can't get safe placements or create a solid anchor, try moving up or down to a better place.

On established big wall routes, you'll

usually find at least one bolt, if not several, at designated belay points. This makes it easy to set up the belay. Bolts next to cracks, which make for excellent belays, are easiest to set up, although bolts aren't always available where you want them. If your pitch ends in a beak seam, you'll find bolts for the anchor. If you come upon a bolted anchor, simply place a carabiner on each bolt, clip in the cordelette, and follow the equalization steps described below.

If you end a pitch where there is only a crack, you will need to create a natural anchor. These are the most common type to make on a wall. Often there's only one crack that runs vertically, and this usually makes for a messy anchor. Ideally, you want the placements more spread out, which streamlines your anchor. Use pitons, stoppers, and cams in the available cracks to create a natural anchor.

More often than not, you'll use a mix of bolts and natural protection to create your anchor. There are several options in such a case. You can use a cordelette to equalize a few bolts and a few pieces of gear. You can use a cordelette on the bolts alone, then equalize two pieces of gear separately, and finally use another sling to equalize both of these. Or you can equalize the bolts with the cordelette and back it up to two or more pieces of gear with a series of clove hitches. It all depends on what you can find for protection and how streamlined you can make your anchor. Above all, make it safe and as efficient as possible to avoid using too much of your rack and to keep it from turning into a mess.

Quite often you'll end a pitch without enough gear to create a belay. If the climbers topo tells you the anchor has bolts, you'll be OK. If it calls for cams, consider leapfrogging those pieces during the pitch till you get a good stopper in, so you can use the cams later for the anchor. Leapfrogging often is needed when you have to build natural anchors; if there are bolts, you usually won't have to do this. For instance, a lot of desert walls have cracks that can be the same size for hundreds of feet, making leapfrogging mandatory unless you have 10 pieces of the same size. This is highly unlikely because it's rather cumbersome to carry that large a rack.

Whether you use bolts, natural features, or a combination, you must create an equalized, multidirectional anchor. To equalize the anchor, you can use a cordelette

KEY EXERCISE: MAKING A POWER POINT

To create an equalized, multidirectional anchor, place a D-shaped carabiner on each piece of gear, then clip a cordelette in to each biner. Make sure one piece of gear can take an upward pull. Pull down the cordelette's slack from in between each piece of gear and grasp all these together so you have a single point from all pieces in the anchor. Tie this point into a figure eight knot. This is the power point.

(ideal) or two or three double-length shoulder slings (not as good, but still works well).

Place an oval or D-shaped (ideal) carabiner on each piece of gear. Clip a cordelette in to each biner, then pull down the slack from in between each piece and grasp all these together so you have a single point from all pieces in the anchor (see Figure 6). Take this point and tie it into a figure eight knot. This is the best single-point anchor you can make. I call it the power point. It's equalized, holds downward multidirectional forces, and holds more than 2000 pounds if the pieces are solidly placed. If you add a piece of gear that can take an upward pull, you'll have a multidirectional power point that can withstand an upward pull, such as in a fall, without failing.

To equalize the pieces using slings, clip one sling in to the two or three pieces, pulling the slack down in between each piece and then making a single twist in each loop of the sling; clip a carabiner in to these points. This creates a downward multidirectional equalized clip-in point. You can tie a knot as you would with cordelette, but there usually isn't enough length in the slings. You can tie a knot at each point that's clipped in to the pieces to remove the chance of the other pieces shock-loading should one fail.

Tying in to the anchor. On a wall climb, the best way to fix the lead line to the anchor is by first giving yourself about 10 feet of slack and then tying in to the power point with a figure eight on a bight.

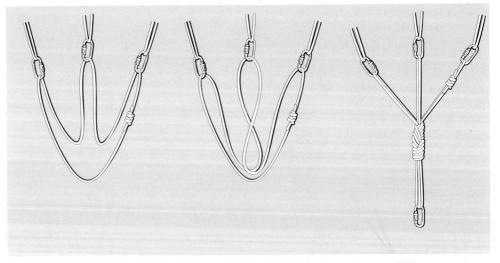

Figure 6. *Static equalization with cordelette: clip cordelette in to three pieces; pull the segments between the pieces down; grasp all of these segments together, tie an overhand or figure eight knot, and clip a locking carabiner in to the loops.*

Having this slack allows you to maneuver around the belay and to haul and access the bags. Use daisy chains to micro-adjust where you want to hang. Also back up the figure eight with a clove hitch clipped in to one of the anchor points above the power point.

Racking at the belay. To keep the extra gear in order at the belay, use one sling to rack cams, stoppers, free carabiners, and quickdraws and another sling for pins, hooks, and other hardware. This way, your belayer can access this gear quickly and simply stuff it into the haul bag when it's not needed.

BELAYING THE LEADER

It can be easy to doze off from fatigue while belaying a leader on a big aid wall where pitches can take hours at a time. If you start to feel like taking a catnap, be sure that you're using an autolocking belay device such as a GriGri; if you're not, tie a knot on the brake-hand side of the belay device a few feet from the device to ensure a safe belay should the leader suddenly fall while you're dreaming about burgers and fries. On a climb on Baffin Island, I belayed Greg Child on a 13-hour lead. I was bored to tears at the hanging belay and found myself drifting in and out of a dream state, only to be woken by the pull on the rope for slack. Luckily, it wasn't Greg falling!

Another important reminder is to always clip a piece of gear in to the anchor as the leader's first piece of protection; never lead directly off a belay, with the rope running from the leader directly to the belayer's belay device without one piece of protection in between the two climbers. If the leader falls directly on your harness early in the pitch without any protection between you, you'll take a direct fall onto your harness. This factor-2 fall could potentially cause you to let go of the brake hand and usually causes injury in some fashion. A factor-2 fall creates the highest impact force on the system, putting excessive stress on the anchor.

TRANSITIONS AT BELAYS

In the typical leading-following process, after the leader has led a pitch and reached the anchor, the leader belays up the second while hauling. The second, meanwhile, follows and cleans the pitch, and then after reaching the anchor, prepares to lead the next pitch. To make the transition at the belay from leading to following to leading faster and easier, follow these steps:

1. When the climber finishes the lead, place the first piece of gear for the new anchor and clip in to it right away, then build the rest of the anchor, equalize it, and use the climber's end of the rope to clip in to the anchor. People have taken falls while placing and equalizing anchors before clipping in.

2. When the second arrives at the belay after following, quickly clip in to the anchor or, better yet, place a piece of gear above the anchor for the start of the next pitch and hang on it while getting the rest of the gear from the new belayer.

3. Once the new leader is hanging on this piece, the new belayer ties a safety knot below the belay device in the rope to free his or her hands for passing gear, etc.

4. The new leader hands off extra gear not needed for the next pitch and anything else, such as a pack and water, to the new belayer.

5. Rehydrate and eat some food while resting for a few minutes before beginning the next pitch. Consult the topo and look ahead to make sure both leader and belayer know where to go.

FOLLOWING

When I started wall climbing, I really didn't know the difference between a jug and a blade: for all I knew, aid climbing had something to do with cutlery. In my ensuing years of scrappiness, I learned just as much following pitches as I did leading them—minus the fear. I quickly learned how to place pins, hooks, and heads better by seeing how my more-experienced partners did things. I also learned a lot from making mistakes. This section shows how to follow pitches, gives tips for cleaning, and describes the different systems used in order to perform them. This way, you won't do the stupid maneuvers I pulled during my early years.

When the leader alerts the second that the leader is almost at the next anchor, the second should start preparations for following. Start tying shoes, shouldering the pack (if there is one), and—as soon as the leader is off belay—breaking down the belay anchor. If there are several pieces in the anchor, take all but two bomber pieces out and clip in to them while waiting to be put on belay. Once you are on belay, you can take out the last pieces and start climbing faster than if you'd waited to remove the entire anchor—this also keeps you from making your partner wait.

Following pitches is relatively fast and easy because you're not hauling or leading hard moves. You can take the back seat and coast up the wall, taking in the views and really letting the whole experience sink in. As you follow, rerack the equipment where you like to have it when you're leading, so when you get to the next anchor you will have most of the rack on you and ready to go for the next lead.

Not all following is easy, though. Some pitches require the follower to perform the same tasks as the leader to ascend the pitch. Jumarring past large roofs, trying to clean a traversing pitch, and following pendulums all take special skills to perform at a fast, safe, and efficient pace. Below are basic methods for following and cleaning.

After that are several ways to set up your jumars and daisy chains for following and cleaning more-difficult terrain. These methods are the best way to clean roofs, traverses, and pendulums. They may seem complicated, but once you get on the rope, it'll feel more intuitive. Read these sections carefully and study the diagrams well so when you do get to one of these situations, you have a visual diagram and process in your mind. Remember to take your time and be safe.

USING ASCENDERS

The second ascends the fixed climbing rope by means that have evolved from the prusik knot to a mechanical device called an ascender to the ultralight ascender called a Tibloc . . . all with the same principle in mind. Jumarring, or jugging, as it's com-

Figure 7. *Prusik setup*

monly called, got its name from a popular mechanical ascender called a Jumar. There are many devices available to ascend a fixed rope with speed and efficiency, and the more ways you know how, the better prepared you'll be should a situation arise in which you need to improvise.

For example, while climbing my first El Capitan route, Zodiak, I dropped a jumar just as I was about to follow pitch 12, the Mark of Zorro: a heinous, steep, zigzagging roof. I was shocked, stunned, and frozen in place at having made such a foolish mistake: I didn't want to tell my partner and spin him into a panic attack too. I rigged a prusik knot and cleaned the pitch using that in tandem with my other jumar. Thankfully, I knew how to use a prusik knot and we finished the climb. The main loss was my expensive jumar.

Mechanical ascenders. The most popular and easiest way to jumar is by using a pair of ascenders. Almost all ascenders have a left- and right-hand model. Clamp both ascenders onto the rope. The ascenders slide up easily, but once they're weighted, the mechanical camming action keeps them from sliding down. Ascenders are simple to use and have made following pitches easy enough that practically anyone can do it.

The crux of using ascenders is setting them up on the daisy chains properly. Getting the correct height from your harness to the device is crucial for smooth operation. For 80 percent of jumarring situations, you'll have one setup that you use as the default setup. The default setup is used on terrain ranging from slabs to vertical. Here's how you establish the default setup (see Figure 8):

1. Decide which hand you want on top (whichever hand is more coordinated) and place that ascender on the rope. Now take a locking carabiner and clip it in to the bottom hole on the ascender.

2. Take one of your two daisy chains and clip it in to the locking carabiner within a few inches of arm's reach. If you clip it too far away, you'll struggle to reach it again once you're hanging on it; too short, and you'll be moving up the rope in short intervals. Make sure the daisy chain isn't twisted when you clip it in. If it's twisted a few

KEY EXERCISE: ASCENDING WITH A PRUSIK KNOT

The prusik knot takes some getting used to, but you absolutely must know how to use it. Using a prusik knot is very simple and it has many uses; however, the main use here is for ascending a fixed rope. This is the old-school way to ascend a rope, but it still works in a pinch. If you're a 007 fan, you might recall Bond taking a spectacular fall off a cliff, only to take his shoelaces off and use them as prusik knots to get back up the rope, kill his enemy, and save the girl. If a prusik knot comes in handy for Bond, it will for you too. A prusik is made with a 4-foot length of 6–7 mm cord tied into a loop with a double fishermans knot. Here's how to set it up:

1. Attach the prusik to the climbing rope by simply folding the loop over the rope and wrapping one end of it around the rope, passing it through the other end of the loop on each pass. After three or four wraps, grab the end that you wrapped around the rope and pull it out away from the rope, pulling the knot tight.

2. Clip in a locking carabiner to this loop and your daisy chain and weight it. The wrapping mechanism locks down on the rope under weight, yet easily slides up the rope when unweighted.

3. Attach a second prusik knot stacked on top of the other to ascend the rope. Clip in an aider with a nonlocking carabiner to each prusik, for your feet (see Figure 7).

4. Adjust the length of the upper daisy chain so the prusik knot is just within arm's reach. Any longer, and you'll struggle to pull yourself up the rope with your arms instead of with the daisy chain.

5. Adjust the length of the lower daisy chain so it is long enough to slide the lower knot freely without tangling in the upper one.

6. Keep tension on the rope as you start out, by holding it down with one hand; otherwise, the prusik knots will just pull up the rope's slack below you.

times, it'll be more difficult to move and will spin the jumar handle around the rope. Make everything clean and clear so it runs smoothly.

3. Repeat steps 1–2 for the lower ascender but make the length slightly longer than for the top one: you won't be hanging on the lower one, so its length isn't as important. The longer you make it, the less chance you have of it getting tangled up or twisted around the other daisy chain.

4. Take a single aider with a nonlocking biner and clip it in to the top ascender, on the locking biner that the daisy chain is clipped to. You don't need a locking biner on the aider. Repeat for the bottom ascender. You

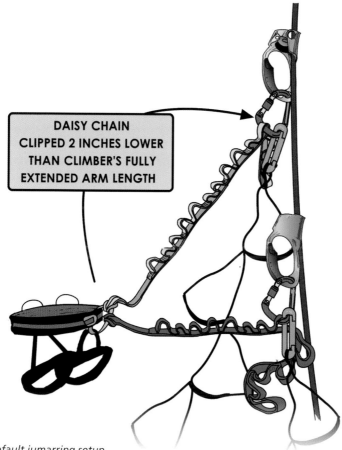

DAISY CHAIN CLIPPED 2 INCHES LOWER THAN CLIMBER'S FULLY EXTENDED ARM LENGTH

Figure 8. *Default jumarring setup*

need to be able to move the aiders on or off the ascenders while jumarring and when you get to the anchor. This is especially true if you have to re-aid-climb a roof.

While ascending lower-angled terrain, put one foot in the third step on the upper

Figure 9. *Frog jumarring system*

ascender's aider and the other foot in the second step on the lower ascender's aider. If you can imagine what it's like to use a Versa-Climber machine in a gym, you'll understand that each foot rises with the same-sided hand to make upward progress. Right hand up, right foot up, then left hand up, left foot up.

On steeper terrain, put one foot in the fourth step on the upper aider and the other foot in the third step on the lower aider. Once you try it, you'll see that this keeps your feet on the same level when the ascenders are about a foot apart, the normal position when jumarring.

Now practice, practice, practice. Getting it set up fast and on the move takes time and practice. The more you do it, the more intuitive it'll become.

Belay device and mechanical ascender. Another alternative for ascending fixed ropes utilizes a GriGri belay device and a single ascender. You can set this system up with a Petzl Traxion and Mini Traxion too. These setups aren't as smooth as using two ascenders, but they work in a pinch and are useful to know. This isn't a good setup for cleaning pitches or traversing fixed ropes, but it serves as another way to ascend a fixed rope.

1. Set up the top ascender in the default mode described above, with two aiders clipped to it as in the Frog system described in the Frog System Key Exercise.
2. Clip the GriGri to your waist harness's belay loop with a locking carabiner and feed the rope coming down from

KEY EXERCISE: ASCENDING WITH THE FROG SYSTEM

The Frog system, as it is commonly called, is another alternative, borrowed from cavers. This is most useful for jugging free-hanging fixed ropes, such as at the start of a steep route or when a party of three has fixed a rope on a steep pitch and the third person jugs the free-hanging rope while the second person cleans the pitch. With the Frog system, you need two ascenders. Here's how to set it up:

1. Clip the lower ascender (a Petzl Croll works best) directly to your waist harness with a locking carabiner; with the biner clipped through the waist belt and the leg loops, clip in the ascender so it rests flat against your belly with the cam facing out.

2. Clip the top hole of the lower ascender to your chest harness. This is what will pull the ascender up as you move. The chest harness might not be perfect for length, but using something you already have cuts down on extra gear. To make the ascender slide up flawlessly each time you move up, make a custom-length sling, use an adjustable sling, or use a shoulder-length sling tied short around your neck to clip in the ascender for the perfect height. I've used a small keychain type biner to clip in the top of the ascender to the chest harness, and it worked like a charm. It doesn't have to be a locking biner because the ascender is locked in to your harness. No aiders or daisy chains are clipped in to this ascender.

3. Set up the top ascender just as in the default setup (see Figure 9), clipped in to the daisy chain but with *both* aiders clipped in to it.

TO ASCEND WITH THE FROG SYSTEM, HERE'S WHAT YOU DO:

1. Put both feet in the third or fourth steps of your aiders (whatever feels right for your height) and push down; put both hands on the upper ascender and pull down—you'll slide up the rope (see Figure 9)

2. At the apex of each movement, push in with your hips and extend your legs straight. As you stand up, the rope slides through the lower jumar.

3. Sit with your weight on the lower ascender, push the upper ascender up the rope, and pull up your legs.

4. Repeat steps 1–3.

To help get started, pinch the rope between your feet; this holds the rope down so it feeds through the lower ascender as you slide up. Once you get about 20 feet up, the rope's weight will self-feed it through the lower ascender.

If you need to rest, the best position is when you're sitting with your weight on the lower ascender with the upper one high on the rope to support your upper body. Let your legs hang out of the aiders.

the upper ascender into it as though you were going to belay.

3. Now take the brake-hand end of the rope and clip it in to a free biner that's clipped on the upper ascender to create a pulleylike mechanism.

To operate, start by sitting on the GriGri and slide the ascender up. Then, as you stand up on the ascender, pull down on the rope through the pulley biner and, at the apex of your movement, let the GriGri take your weight again. Repeat this process.

BASIC CLEANING TIPS

Now that you have learned the different jumarring setups, here are some tricks that will help you become more efficient at cleaning pitches.

Cleaning the anchor. Once you have the jugs on the rope and are ready to leave the belay, take a sling and clip in to a piece in the anchor that'll be last to come out, such as a cam. This will keep you connected to the anchor as you pull the slack out of the rope with the jumars. Once you start moving up, clean the anchor. On overhanging pitches, stay clipped in to the last piece so you can clean the anchor without swinging out into space.

Passing a piece of gear. As you get to a piece of gear, slide the top jug up until it hits the biner on the piece and then bring the lower jug up high under it. Now take the top jug off the rope while standing on the lower aider, clip it above the piece of gear, and sit in your harness on it. With the piece between both jumars, you have both hands free to remove it. You can leave the piece of gear clipped in to the lead rope as you remove it, which serves as a backup should it pop out unexpectedly. If it's a piton, move the lower jug past it too by unclipping the piece of gear and sliding the jug up so you have more room to work. It's best to have the piton about waist high so you can wield the hammer without the rope and aiders getting in the way.

Here's a way to get past a piece without taking your jugs off the rope. First slide the jugs up to the piece of gear and unclip the gear from the rope with your lower jug hand. Then, while holding onto the piece's biner with your lower hand, slide the top jug up the rope and sit on it. Now you can easily remove the piece of gear. This works well on slabs and vertical terrain and eliminates having to remove the jug from the rope.

Reracking. When you're cleaning, always rerack the equipment as you go so it's ready for the next lead. The idea is to streamline the rack as you go so it's not a rat's nest when you arrive at the belay. You and your partner should decide ahead of time how you're going to rack the gear and then stick to that plan the entire route. This helps the rack stay organized in the same fashion no matter who's got it.

- Put stoppers back on one biner, cams on a single biner, and pins of the same style on separate biners: blades with blades, angles with angles, etc.
- If one piece of gear has a sling or quickdraw on it, take off the sling and rack it with the slings, putting the piece of gear where it belongs. Clip quickdraws to the side of your harness.

If a pin has keeper slings or was tied off, put the tie-off on one biner and the pin on the pin biner.

Cleaning pitons. Piton removal can sometimes be difficult. To help keep your pins from falling to the ground while you're cleaning them, clip in a cleaner biner or a funkness device that you either hold or clip in to the rope. Pull out on the pin as you whack it with the hammer to help remove it. In general, hit the pin up and down (mostly up, to keep from scarring the placement) till it's loose enough to pull out with the funkness device. The funkness device is the best way to pull pins. Just clip one end in to the head of your hammer and the other in to the pin and then yank it out.

If the pin is in an expanding flake, you might have to expand the flake with a larger pin. An expanding flake tends to pinch a thin pin badly, so expanding the flake makes a stuck pin come out more easily. Hammer in a larger pin near the one you're cleaning to get it out, then remove the larger one.

Blades can be stubborn because they bend and conform to the rock, so you might have to work on them longer.

For micropitons, it's much better to tap up and down on them till they're loose enough to remove with your hand. If you funk them out, they often break and usually scar the rock or, even worse, destroy the placement. Take the time to gently remove them because they are fragile.

Don't clean copper heads. They always scar the rock when cleaned, leading to further damage and often destroying a dubious placement. Once a head is placed, it's not worth removing because it conformed to that specific placement and won't work in a different one. Leave them fixed for future parties. You'll find most heads fixed on trade routes.

Cleaning clean-aid devices. Stoppers, once they are weighted, can be really hard to clean. Use a nut tool and tap up on the stopper with a hammer. If a stopper is really welded, try pulling up on it with a funkness device and a hammer or tapping it with a Lost Arrow. When cleaning microstoppers and RPs, don't pull up on them hard or use a funkness device because it can easily break the cable. Instead, tap upward with the cleaning tool and hammer. You can use a nut tool and a piton as extensions to your fingers for hard-to-reach stoppers that are loose but need to be turned or pulled up to get free.

Camming devices are easier to clean because they operate with a trigger, which can be used to remove them. If they get flipped upside down or get shoved deep into a crack, use a nut tool that has a hook on the end to pull on the trigger to free it. If it's really deep, use two nut tools or a pin and a nut tool, pushing on the stem with one while pulling on the trigger with the other. If a cam is overcammed and stuffed into a crack that's too tight for it and you can't pull on the trigger to free it, use a hammer and gently tap it sideways out of the crack. Sometimes cams get stuffed in too deep or simply get stuck and remain there for years. It's better to leave a fixed cam in place than to beat on it till it's damaged and worthless.

Slider nuts can be hard to clean. Don't use a funkness device on them because it will break the cable. Instead, work the slider nut back and forth using the trigger till it comes loose, then pull on the trigger and remove it. In expanding flakes, you might have to weight the piece above or below it to get it free. They are fragile and you need to have patience to remove them without damaging them. If they're really stuck, tap a pin on the fixed side and work the stem back and forth.

FOLLOWING AND CLEANING OVERHANGS AND ROOFS

When the terrain is overhanging and the rope is free-hanging, there are better ways to ascend the rope. One alternative is to use the default setup mentioned above in a different way. This works great for jugging fixed ropes and for following overhanging pitches.

1. Clip in both aiders to the lower ascender and use both feet to push.
2. While pushing with your feet, hold onto the lower ascender and push the upper ascender as far as you can reach, then immediately sit in your harness on the upper ascender (a good example of the reason for making sure the upper daisy is set just right).
3. Now slide the lower ascender up while lifting your feet in the aiders.
4. Repeat steps 2–3. You'll resemble a caterpillar inching up a rope and get a massive abdominal workout.

Cleaning pitches that climb through roofs is strenuous. Here is how you clean them.

1. Slide your jumars up to the piece. While standing in the lower aider and holding onto the lower jumar, pass the upper one past the piece and hang on it.
2. Use your upper hand to pull tension on the rope below the lower jumar while using your other hand to release the cam on that jumar. Now let some rope pass through the lower jumar so you're hanging on the upper one right under the next piece in the roof.
3. Pass the lower jumar by the lower piece and move up. Now you can clean the piece you just passed.

If the pieces in the roof have been extended by the leader to allow the rope to run clean and without rope drag, it'll be a long reach for you to clean the pieces. Solve this problem by taking an aider and clipping in to the piece above it so you can get closer to the wall and clean it. You might have to re-aid-climb sections in a roof when it's too difficult to clean it on the jumars. If this is the case, keep sliding up both jumars as you re-aid the section; in case a piece blows, you're caught by the jumars. While cleaning roofs, frequently tie backup figure eight on a bight knots and clip them in to a locking carabiner on your belay loop.

TENSION TRAVERSES AND PENDULUMS

Tension traverses and pendulums offer two ways of reaching other features like ledges and cracks that are otherwise inaccessible.

Follow these steps to perform and clean them without a fuss.

Executing a tension traverse or a pendulum is simple. For a tension traverse, the leader calls for tension, leans back on the rope, and uses rope tension in combination with the rock features to cross a blank section. To execute a pendulum, the leader also calls for tension, leans back on the rope, but gets lowered to a point where he or she is able to reach the next crack at the apex of the swing after running back and forth below his or her pendulum point. Once a leader has completed his or her pendulum or tension traverse, he or she must continue climbing higher. The best plan is to climb as high as is safely possible before placing protection. This reduces rope drag, and protects the second from a long fall.

The piece of gear used for the pendulum point isn't always retrievable but if the rope runs free well above the pendulum point, the second may be able to retrieve the piece and swing over. If, however, the rope is dangerously horizontal or runs downward the second will need to lower from the same anchor and leave the piece behind. The choice of cleaning method depends on the amount of rope you have with you compared to the length of the pendulum. The loop method is faster but more dangerous. The following tips will help you rig and clean these moves without a fuss.

Cleaning Short Pendulums: The Loop Method.

1. Jumar to the leader's pendulum point, clip a figure eight on a bight below the jumars into your belay loop with a locking biner, then clip directly into the pendulum point.

2. Take the loop of rope hanging below your backup knot, make a bight, and feed it through the biner or sling that you will leave on the pendulum point. Clip it to a biner on your belay loop, pulling it tight so your weight shifts onto it.

3. Unclip both the rope with your jumars on it and the direct clip-in point from the pendulum point, and lower yourself out with the loop of rope running through the biner or sling, using your hand as a brake to control the speed.

4. As you lower out, your jumars take your weight as you reach the end of the pendulum.

5. Back on your jumars, unclip the bight of rope and pull it through the piece to free it.

This loop method can work for longer pendulums if you have enough rope for four strands (the two doubled lengths) to reach from the pendulum point to the fall line point (end of swing—or close enough to let go and ride!) and, if you're confident you can hold yourself freehand. You may not want to risk it, however, even if the swing is short: in that case, you'll want to rappel.

Cleaning Long Pendulums. There are two rappel methods; the first uses the rope you're jumarring on, the second using a second rope.

1. Jumar up to the pendulum point and clip directly into it.

2. Tie a figure eight on a bight under your jumars and clip it into your belay loop with a locking biner.

3. Untie from the end of the rope and feed it through the pendulum point and back to a rappel device on the belay loop, pulling it tight and shifting your weight onto the rappel. This is similar to the short method but this rappel uses two strands instead of four.

4. Unclip both the lead line with the jumars on it and the direct clip-in from the pendulum point, and feed out slack with your brake hand until your jumars take your weight.

5. Remove the rope from the rappel device and pull the rope through the pendulum point to free it. Tie back into the end and continue cleaning.

You need a second length of rope brought specifically for cleaning pendulums for this second method. Use this one when you need to clean a long pendulum at the beginning of a pitch and you don't have enough rope for the other methods.

1. Jumar to the pendulum point and clip into it directly, with a backup knot clipped into the belay loop as described above.

2. Feed the second rope through the point so it's an equal length doubled-strand, and set up a rappel.

3. Shift your weight onto the rappel and unclip the lead rope and the direct clip-in point. Lower out with your brake hand until you reach the end of the pendulum and pull the rope through the point to free it.

Check and double-check your systems before committing to these steps. Take your time as they are complicated and take practice to master.

HAULING

On any wall climb, you'll be hauling at least some food and water. Add gear for a bivy, and suddenly hauling becomes a major chore.

PACKING HAUL BAGS

Often, a lot of gear goes into the haul bag, so it's important to pack it efficiently. This makes it simple to access what you need, when you need it, while protecting what's in the bag from the rough ride up the wall. Packing haul bags is basically the same for any load, whether for a long free route or a multiday nail-up.

Light loads. If the load is light, use a sleek little pack or haul bag designed for just this purpose. If you plan to jumar with the pack on your back, it doesn't matter too much how you pack its contents because it won't get banged around much.

Heavy items such as water go in the bottom, with extra clothing and food above. A hydration system works great because the container collapses as the water is consumed, making more room in the pack. Similar are collapsing water bottles.

Medium loads. If you plan on a one- to two-day route, you'll have a larger haul bag.

1. Start by lining the bag with a pad, such as a sleeping pad.
2. Put your water in the bottom vertically so it doesn't poke out into the side of the bag.
3. Put your sleeping bag in next since it'll come out at the end of the day.
4. Pad canned food and pack it vertically near the middle to avoid ruining a brand-new haul bag in one haul.
5. Organize food in small to medium-size stuff sacks, and put them above the water so they don't get crushed or wet.
6. On top, put extra clothes, headlamps, and other essentials you want quick access to, such as candy, gum, a hat, or sunblock.
7. Use an extra shirt or clothing to pad the top of the bag, which helps prevent wear and tear on the haul bag's material.

Heavy loads. If you're doing a multiday wall, using two half-empty bags instead of one overstuffed bag allows you to dig into each bag for what you need without having to unpack all the contents and clip them randomly in to the anchor, which increases the chance of dropping something. Keep all your personal things in one bag so you know where all your belongings are when you get to the bivy. Use a medium-size bag for the sleeping bags, most of the water and food, and extra clothing; use another smaller bag for the day's rations of food, water, and whatever else you want on hand, such as a camera. This way, you can clip the light bag under the big one for easy access during the day

without having to dig through the full supply.

To line all of a tall bag, stack two pads on top of each other, but if you can't line the whole bag, the lower half is more important. Pack larger bags the same as you would a smaller one. Most bags today have at least one or two zippered pockets on the inside near the top to keep loose items such as lip balm, a topo, sunglasses, etc., easy to organize. Keeping everything organized in the bags makes it much faster to settle into a bivy when you're tired and want nothing more than to crack open a tall cool one while nibbling on some food.

TYING THE ROPE TO THE HAUL BAGS

For most hauling situations, tie the haul rope directly in to the haul-bag straps, using a figure eight follow-through, to simplify the system. If you use a locking carabiner to clip the bags to the haul line, tie a figure eight on a bight, making the loop as small as possible: if it's tied in a long loop, when the knot reaches the hauling system the bags can be left hanging too far below the pulley for its daisy chain or leash to reach the anchor.

Today's haul bags often have straps of two different lengths to haul from. The difference in length is about as long as a biner. The reason for this is so when the longer strap is tied to the haul line, the shorter strap is clipped in to the tie-in knot. This allows the shorter strap to be unclipped so the bag hangs on the longer strap, allowing you unencumbered access to the bag. When the short strap is clipped back in, the bag hangs properly for hauling.

Protect the knot on the haul line by using any plastic beverage container cut off about 4 inches from the top; they're cheap and work great. Before attaching the bags, slide the haul line down through the container's mouthpiece, with the mouth opening facing up so it covers the knot. These are usually good for one or two walls.

Modern haul bags are equipped with comfortable carrying straps and a removable waist belt. Before leaving the ground, remove the waist belt and pack it away in a compartment in the bottom of the bag for sleek hauling on route, and tuck away the shoulder straps to keep them from getting damaged during hauling. If you don't have to walk off the route and can rappel, you can remove the carrying system before leaving the ground, to reduce weight on the descent.

HOW HAULING SYSTEMS WORK

The ability to raise loads with a rope is increased when the rope is used in conjunction with a pulley or pulleys. Combinations of fixed and moving pulleys create systems that multiply the force that climbers are able to apply. The resulting mechanical advantage of using pulley systems enables a climber to lift a load by applying less force, over a longer distance.

Pulley systems can be divided into three categories: simple, compound, and complex. For most wall climbing applications you only need a simple pulley system; the exception is the Spanish Burton, which is a commonly used complex 3:1 system. While there are other compound and complex systems, they are used exclusively for rescues and so aren't discussed in this book.

The simplest example of a pulley system is the 1:1. Here the pulley provides no mechanical advantage but rather only changes the direction of pull. The force required to lift the load is approximately equal to the load itself, and the amount of rope brought in is equal to the distance the load is raised.

Mechanical advantage comes into effect in a simple system when a pulley is added to the system; that is, a pulley that moves toward the anchor as the load is raised. This is the case in the simple 3:1 hauling system. The price of the mechanical advantage gained from the moving pulley is an increase in the distance you have to pull the rope. In the case of the 3:1, you have to pull in three times the amount of rope on the pull side to raise the load a certain distance; only a third of the force is required, however.

Finally, the Spanish Burton represents a complex 3:1 pulley system because the traveling pulley moves toward the load instead of toward the anchor, as in the simple 3:1 system. The mechanical advantage is the same. The Spanish Burton is a complex pulley system that is practical for hauling loads while wall climbing.

BASICS OF HAULING

Methods for hauling equipment up steep walls used to involve simply dragging a pack or bag up hand over hand, pitch by pitch. Once climbers started to ascend the larger faces of sheer cliffs, new ways of

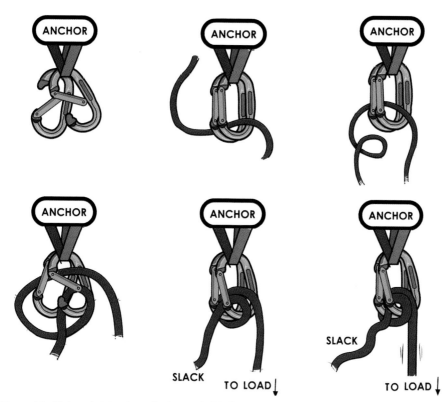

Figure 10. *Alpine clutch, also called a garda hitch*

hauling were developed. After all, necessity is the mother of invention. Today, modern pulleys and hauling devices are compact, lightweight, and easy to use, changing the way we look at hauling. This section shows you how to set up several different hauling systems.

On every haul, make sure that the hauling point (anchor) is equalized and can't be shock-loaded if one piece pulls. In any hauling situation, have the pulley as high as possible so when the bags arrive,

you can clip them to the anchor at a convenient height for access. If the pulley is too low and the knot jams into it, the bags will hang far below the anchor and you'll have to climb down to them to get something from them. No matter which system you use, as you haul, stack the haul rope for the next pitch.

With really heavy loads it's best to use a 3:1. You could haul twice, but that takes twice as long and it's also more complicated because you have to send back the haul line for the second load. This can be remedied if you have two haul ropes, but again, this adds more weight, gear, confusion, and time than it's worth.

GARDA HITCH METHOD

The garda hitch (also called an alpine clutch) is a useful hauling method on alpine or long free climbs when you might need to haul a light pack and didn't bring a pulley. It's a fast, simple, and effective pulley system with minimal equipment necessary. Set it up as follows:

1. Clip two identical oval carabiners in to the anchor, with both gates on the same side but opening in opposite directions (see Figure 10).
2. Clip the rope in to both biners.
3. Make a loop in the rope and clip the loop in to the biner on the weight side allowing the end you will pull on to fall in between the two biners.
4. To raise the weight, pull on the free end of the rope. Once you stop pulling, the two biners pinch together, locking the load in place. The rope pulls in only one direction.
5. To unlock the hitch, pull on the free end till the biners separate, then place another biner or a nut tool between them to keep them apart and transfer the load to where you want it.

1:1 MECHANICAL ADVANTAGE HAULING SYSTEMS

The 1:1 is the most basic hauling setup. This is the fastest way to haul a load that's less than or equal to your body weight. It requires the use of a pulley which creates a change of direction in the system and allows for a low friction pull. This is the standard setup for counterweight hauling systems for one or two people. Counterweight 1:1 hauling is really useful when you are starting out on a long climb, when the bags are heaviest. It's faster than the 3:1, so if you decide to haul twice, 1:1 is best.

You move the bags up either by using a single pulley with an inverted jumar or by using a combo device (the best way) attached to the anchor and counterweighting the load. Make sure when counterweight

A simple 1:1 hauling setup using a combo device

Setting up an alpine clutch. Top left: *step 1, clip the rope in to both biners.* Bottom left: *step 2, loop the rope under both biners and clip the pulling end in to the first biner so it hangs between both biners.* Top right: *step 3, pull on the rope in between the biners to haul.* Bottom right: *step 4, when you let go of the rope, the biners are pinched together locking it in place.*

127

hauling that you're backed up with a safety leash to the anchor; don't rely solely on the haul line and jumars. Here's how to set up the 1:1 hauling system:

1. Back up the pulley system using locking biners to clip one end of the sling to the loaded rope just below the pulley and the other end to an anchor point (see Figure 11). Should an anchor point fail or the pulley break, the load will be caught.

2. Lengthen both daisy chains to full length so you can haul about 3 feet at a time till they stop you from lowering farther, then clip them both to an

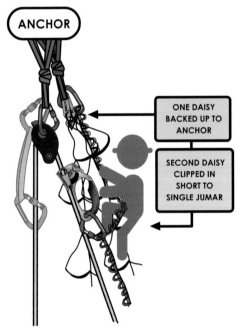

Figure 11. *Hauling with a 1:1 mechanical advantage*

ONE DAISY BACKED UP TO ANCHOR

SECOND DAISY CLIPPED IN SHORT TO SINGLE JUMAR

anchor point. Place one jumar on the rope between you and the pulley. If you want to go down farther, use the lead rope as your daisy chain and adjust it to whatever length you want. Remember that you'll have to jumar back up to reset the haul each time.

3. While standing in the aiders that are clipped in to the anchor, use your weight to hoist the load by sliding the jumar up to the pulley and pulling down on it with your weight; the movement is like doing squats in the gym, but you're standing in your aiders.

4. To increase the haul, pull up on the load with one hand as you counterweight it by pulling down on the jumar with your weight simultaneously. This is really effective when the load is slightly heavier than you: when you counterweight it and pull up on the load, you drop down almost effortlessly as the bag quickly moves up. You can do this for the entire length of the haul if you have another rope, such as another lead line, to use as backup.

5. Once your daisy chains and/or the lead rope stop you, slide the jumar back up while you stand up in the aiders.

6. Repeat steps 3–5.

Counterweight 1:1 hauling can also be done with two people: an important reminder is to have a bombproof anchor when performing a two-person counterweight haul.

1. After cleaning the pitch, the second will back him- or herself up to the anchor with a 50-foot length of the lead rope (or whatever length he or

she is comfortable with) and attach him- or herself to the haul rope with daisy chains to jumars under the top climber (see Figure 12).

2. While the top person is on a short leash (daisy chains) to the anchor and performs a regular body haul, the lower person acts as deadweight and is lowered as the bags move up.

3. Once the bottom person comes tight on the leash, he or she jugs back up and the process is repeated.

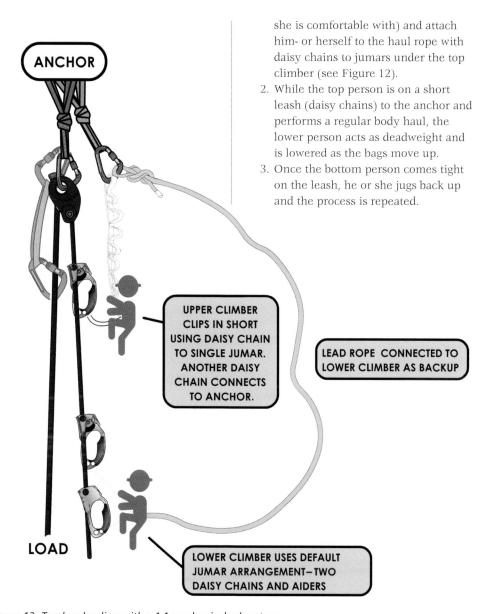

ANCHOR

UPPER CLIMBER CLIPS IN SHORT USING DAISY CHAIN TO SINGLE JUMAR. ANOTHER DAISY CHAIN CONNECTS TO ANCHOR.

LEAD ROPE CONNECTED TO LOWER CLIMBER AS BACKUP

LOAD

LOWER CLIMBER USES DEFAULT JUMAR ARRANGEMENT—TWO DAISY CHAINS AND AIDERS

Figure 12. *Tandem hauling with a 1:1 mechanical advantage*

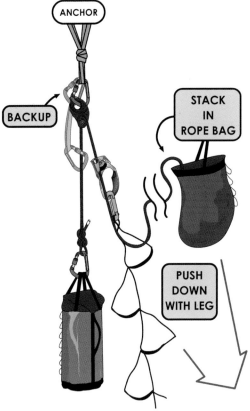

Figure 13. *Leg hauling with a 1:1 mechanical advantage*

Leg haul setup using a combo device

4. As the top person hauls the bags, the lower person can jumar in place to get the same effect.

Counterweight hauling is also easily performed in a party of three. The third person counterweights the leader's haul as the second cleans the pitch. The third person has to jug a fixed free rope to get to the anchor first, but this is a great way to move quickly and to share the burden.

LEG HAULING WITH A 1:1 MECHANICAL ADVANTAGE

For hauling light loads, leg hauling is the best way to go.

1. Set up the haul with a 1:1 mechanical advantage as described above, and clip one aider in to the hauling jumar (see Figure 13).
2. Stand in this aider and simply push down with your leg to raise the load.

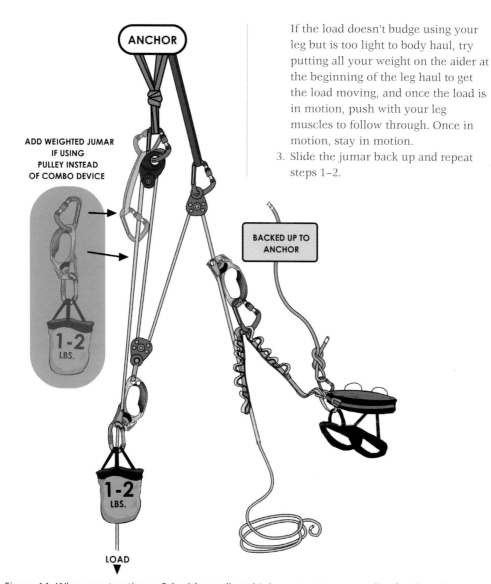

If the load doesn't budge using your leg but is too light to body haul, try putting all your weight on the aider at the beginning of the leg haul to get the load moving, and once the load is in motion, push with your leg muscles to follow through. Once in motion, stay in motion.

3. Slide the jumar back up and repeat steps 1–2.

ANCHOR

ADD WEIGHTED JUMAR
IF USING
PULLEY INSTEAD
OF COMBO DEVICE

BACKED UP TO ANCHOR

1-2
LBS.

1-2
LBS.

LOAD
▼

Figure 14. *When constructing a 3:1 with a redirect it's important to use a pulley for the redirect instead of a biner. You lose up to 40 percent of the efficiency due to the friction created by the rope running over it.*

A 3:1 system with a redirect

3:1 MECHANICAL ADVANTAGE HAULING SYSTEMS

To move a heavier load without much effort, use the 3:1 mechanical advantage hauling system with a redirect. This is more complex and takes more time to set up and haul than a 1:1 system. The 3:1 sets up like this:

1. Feed the rope through a combo device or pulley and clip the device or pulley in to the power point (anchor) with a locking carabiner (see Figure 14). This allows the device or pulley to rotate as you haul. Don't clip the device or pulley directly to a bolt.

2. Attach an inverted jumar to the loaded rope and clip it in to the same anchor point with a sling or quickdraw (this step is not necessary with a combo device). Add weight to keep it in place; otherwise, it'll move up as the haul rope moves. This jumar will lock down on the load after it's raised.

3. Attach a second inverted jumar to the load rope 2 feet below the combo device or pulley, and attach another pulley to this jumar. Also add weight to this second jumar.

4. Feed the haul rope coming out of the combo device or first pulley through this second pulley.

5. Now redirect the haul rope through a quickdraw, sling, or small pulley attached to the anchor. This is where you'll pull down. Use a jumar attached directly to your harness to pull down on the rope.

6. You'll be able to pull the bags up 2 feet till the lower inverted jumar

moves up against the combo device or first pulley. At this point, stand back up in your aiders, slide the lower inverted jumar back down 2 feet, and slide the jumar on your harness back up.

7. Repeat steps 5–6 until the bags reach the anchor.

A variation to the 3:1 hauling system is called the Spanish Burton or the ratchet; it requires only one extra pulley to set up. Basically, this 3:1 system acts on the loaded

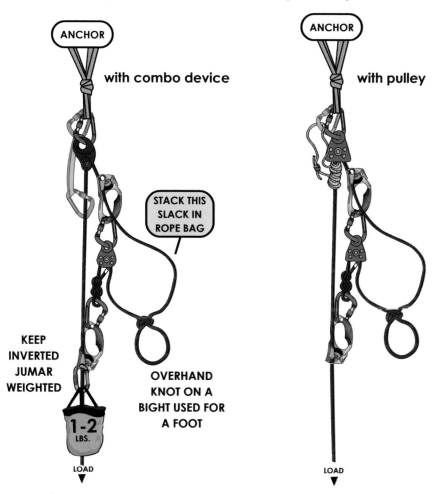

Figure 15. *Spanish Burton 3:1 variation: with a combo device; with a pulley*

A 3:1 using the Spanish Burton setup

rope, allowing you to keep the system set up and ready for the next haul, reducing setup time. You use your leg to haul instead of your body. This is how you set it up:

1. Set up the haul rope through a combo device (see Figure 15) or through a pulley and inverted jumar on the anchor (see Figure 15), as you would for steps 1–2 of the 3:1 hauling system described above.
2. Attach an inverted jumar to the loaded rope, with weight on the jumar, as in step 3 of the 3:1 hauling system described above, but don't attach a pulley to this jumar.
3. Clip the end of the haul rope to this jumar using a locking biner.
4. Now attach another jumar, in the normal up position, to the haul rope coming out of the first pulley.
5. Connect a pulley to this second jumar, using a locking carabiner, and run the rope up through this pulley.
6. On the rope about 3 feet below the second pulley, tie an overhand knot on a bight with a loop big enough for your foot.
7. Step into this loop and push down on it. The load will lift as you push down with your foot.
8. To reset the system, simply slide the second pulley and your foot up at the same time to the start position.

You can continue adding mechanical advantage with the 5:1 and 7:1 pulley systems; however, they require more equipment, are more time consuming to set up, and are used more in rescue applications than for simply hauling bags. To learn more about these systems, refer to one of the many books published on rescue and self-rescue.

LOWERING OUT THE BAGS

On traversing pitches, the haul line will pull the haul bags off to either side, making it nearly impossible to unweight them from the anchor so you can release them for hauling. To release them, you have to do a minihaul with a lower-out line. If you don't do this, the bags will cut loose and swing out in space. This endangers your gear—water bottles and other fragile items can get crushed—but, more important, the bags could get stuck on a flake or in a crack at the far end of the pendulum swing, leaving you with a nearly impossible retrieval. It also spins the haul line, and it is more difficult to haul the bags when they're swinging out in space.

I'll admit to nearly losing all our gear when I didn't lower out the haul bags on a traversing pitch up high on Wall of Early Morning Light on El Capitan. The bags were light enough to lift with my arms off the belay, and I forgot to clip them in short to give myself some rope to lower them out with. When my partner said he was ready to haul, I unclipped the pigs and let 'em rip. They dropped down into space in a fantastic arc, swinging on the rope with great speed. Instantly I realized I hadn't cinched the top closed, and I watched aghast as they violently slammed into the wall several times before the swinging ended. Fortunately, nothing fell out and the bags didn't rip apart, which would have sent all our precious gear thousands of feet to the valley floor. If we'd lost our gear, we would've been in a world of hurt.

On traverses and overhangs, always lower out the bags. You can either use the haul line, unless it's a full rope-length haul, or use another rope for just this purpose. If you know there will be a lot of lowers, bring a 40-foot piece of 7 mm rope for a lower-out line. Petzl makes the Swivel, a device that keeps your rope from spinning, which is very handy on traversing hauls. Here's how to haul the bags off the belay with either the remaining haul line or the lower-out line:

1. If using the remaining length of the haul line, tie a figure eight on a bight in the rope and clip it in to the haul bags with a locking carabiner. If using a separate lower-out line, simply tie the rope to the bags.

2. Clip the rope through a directional piece such as a quickdraw on the anchor above the bags and then pass the rope down through your belay device on your harness (see Figure 16).

3. When the bags are ready to be hauled from above, use your weight to lift the bags off the anchor so their weight is on the belay device.

4. Unclip the bags from the anchor and slowly lower them out till they're directly under the haul point or until you run out of line. At this point, the climber above hauls the bags after you have removed the lower-out line from your belay device and let the

Figure 16. *Lowering out a haul bag: the setup; the lower.*

rope hang on the load. Even if you can't lower the bags all the way out, it's better than just cutting them loose.

Alternatively, when the bags arrive at the belay, you can set up a Münter-mule knot as the clip-in point: you won't have to do a minihaul to get the bags off the anchor. Here's how you set it up:

1. Tie the lower-out line in to the bags on the ground, or leave a 20-foot tail of free rope on the haul line and clip the bags in short on a figure eight on a bight with a locking carabiner (see Figure 17).

2. When the bags get to the anchor, clip the lower-out line or the tail of extra haul rope in to a locking biner on the

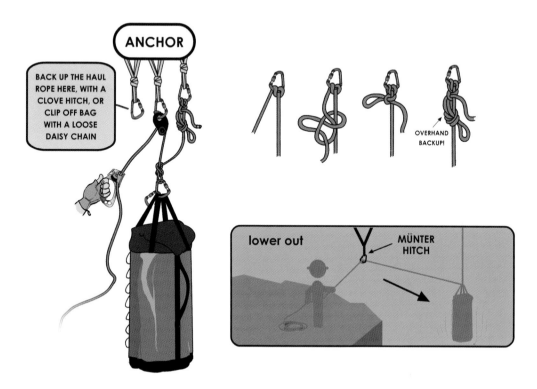

ANCHOR

BACK UP THE HAUL ROPE HERE, WITH A CLOVE HITCH, OR CLIP OFF BAG WITH A LOOSE DAISY CHAIN

OVERHAND BACKUP!

lower out

MÜNTER HITCH

Figure 17. *Using a Münter-mule knot to lower out haul bags: raise the bag to the anchor; tie the Münter knot; tie the mule knot; slide the mule knot up tight to the Münter knot; tie an overhand knot for backup; lower out the haul bag on just the Münter knot.*

anchor above the pulley, using a Münter knot. Pull the knot tight against the bags.

3. With the slack end of the rope, tie a mule knot around the rope leading to the bags, then slide it up tight against the Münter knot (see Figure 17). Make the loop in the mule knot long

enough so you can tie an overhand knot on the rope as a backup.

4. Haul the bags just enough so you can release the haul system and lower the bags onto the Münter-mule knot.

5. Back up the knot by clipping the haul line in to another point in the anchor or with a leash tied in to the haul

bags; use a daisy chain girth-hitched to the haul-bag straps so when they get to an anchor, you can easily clip them in at any height.

6. Now you can take apart the old haul system.

7. On the next haul, the bags are ready to be released and lowered without having to do a minihaul. When the haul line starts pulling the bags up, remove the backup overhand knot and the mule knot, and lower out the bags on the Münter hitch (see Figure 17).

PASSING KNOTS

If you've fixed a few pitches on a route by tying two or more ropes together, you'll probably be hauling the bags on them too. You'll have to pass the knot while hauling. Here's how to do it with lighter loads:

1. Haul the load till the knot is just below the pulley system. Use either a prusik knot or another ascender attached to the haul line below the knot to hold the bags in place. If you're using a pulley and two jumars to haul, just let the bags hang on the lower jumar.

2. Remove the haul rope from the pulley.

3. Now clip the haul rope through a biner at least 1 foot above the pulley, and haul the bags through the biner until the knot is above the pulley.

4. With the bags being held by the lower ascender, you can use the slack to reassemble the pulley system and continue hauling.

If the bags are heavy, you'll have to lower the hauling point because it's too hard to haul a heavy load through a biner. Here's how:

1. Again, haul the load till the knot is just below the pulley or combo device hauling system. If you're using a combo device, place a prusik knot or a jumar below the knot to hold the load while you transfer it. Attach the prusik knot or jumar at least 2 feet lower than the original haul point so you have enough slack in the haul line to reassemble the new haul point lower than the knot (see Figure 18).

2. Lower the pulley or combo device to a point where it will pass the knot (see Figure 18).

3. Reassemble the haul and continue hauling. You'll have to lower yourself as well so you can continue body hauling.

ROPE MANAGEMENT

There's just about nothing worse than getting rope tangled into an endless mess that eats up time and burns out your patience. Managing your ropes carefully will make for a faster transition, whether you're belaying, jumarring, or hauling. Keep your anchors visibly clear, with ropes stacked, gear neatly racked, and everything ready for the next move.

When you're hauling bags, it's nice to take a break between every 40–50 feet of rope that's pulled up. Use this time to neatly stack the rope, keeping it from getting tangled with all the other gear, from

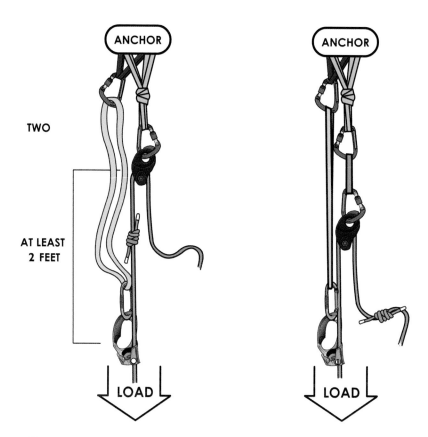

Figure 18. *Passing a knot while hauling a heavy load: once the knot reaches the haul point, place an inverted jumar or prusik knot on the haul line at least 2 feet lower than the original haul point and allow it to hold the load; once the original haul point is dismantled, extend it with a sling and reassemble it just above the jumar or prusik knot—now you have passed the knot and can continue hauling.*

snagging on flakes or knobs below, and free of getting tangled in the wind around other equipment. Believe me, I've spent hours denoodling ropes that somehow tied themselves in knots and looped through just about everything in sight. There are several options for stacking a rope.

- A rope bucket is very handy, but it is an extra piece of gear you don't really need.
- Metolius makes the Rope Hook, a simple hook that clips in to the anchor and that you flake the rope over.
- You can tie an overhand knot on a bight with the rope you want to stack

and feed loops through it and stack it that way.

- You can also stack a rope in a shoulder sling or a leg loop in an aider.
- You can stack it over your daisy chain and, when you're done, use a shoulder sling looped around it and clip it in to the anchor.
- You can stack the rope on the haul bag, too, but this makes it nearly impossible to access the bag.
- If you have a portaledge set up, just stack the rope right there as if the ledge were the ground.

RETREATING AND DESCENDING

At some point, you might have to rappel your route for the descent or a retreat off a climb due to bad weather, time pressures, lack of food or experience, or injury—or because you just can't climb with your partner anymore. Whatever the reason, you have to know how to get down safely with all your gear. This is an overwhelming task, considering the amount of gear that wall climbing requires, especially when you have to rappel thousands of feet down roofs, across pendulums, and back across traverses. Once you've climbed a route beyond the halfway mark, retreating may be more work than sitting out a storm and finishing the climb. Very rarely is a route arrow straight, with a ledge every 200 feet with perfect cracks for creating rappel anchors. Quite often, retreating takes place in the dark, during a storm, or when one person is injured and incapable of helping.

Magnify these problems by the ropes getting caught in a crack or over a flake when you pull on them, sometimes forcing you to cut precious length off them or to reload a pitch to free them. This can cause you to make more anchors, depleting your gear resources and making retreat even more difficult. It's downright scary business. No matter how you slice it, it's a serious task and the better prepared you are, the better off you'll be.

I've left hordes of gear on new routes in the Himalaya because when you climb a new route, there are no fixed anchors. One route in particular stands out. It was the first ascent of the northwest face of Great Trango Tower in Pakistan, a 6000-foot granite wall topping out at more than 20,000 feet. After reaching the summit, we looked at our rack and how far we had to rappel and wondered whether we'd have enough gear to make it. Our pin rack was destroyed from the climb, and we had to rappel into the unknown because our route had traversed over big roofs and would be too difficult to descend.

After having made a 24-hour push to the summit from our last high point, we started the descent in the dark in one of the worst storms of the climb. On the second rappel, when we pulled our two ropes, one of them caught. I jumared the rope, backed up by another dynamic rope, till I could free it from a flake, and we continued down. Everything was soaked, but the worst part of the descent didn't happen until the middle of the night.

The three of us—Alex Lowe, Mark Synnott, and I—hanging in a vertical river in freezing temperatures in unknown territory, were praying we would find cracks in which to make anchors. We had four haul bags and three guys on the anchors, so those anchors had to be solid . . . but we couldn't afford to leave too much gear because if we used it all too early, we might not reach the ground. We didn't have any bolts for hand-drilling an anchor if there were no cracks to use, so we were at the mercy of the wall.

Halfway down, Mark was swinging from side to side at the end of the ropes with the knots jammed in his rappel device, and he was looking for anything to make an anchor in. He eventually found a huge loose flake off to the side that, when he hit it with his fist, made a spooky bongo sound, vibrating into the stormy night. There were no other options. As we all hung there on wide cams flexing out the flake under the load, we prayed it would hold and then pulled the ropes from above: our only backup should the flake jettison itself into the blackness.

The anchor held. Several more times, the ropes snagged in cracks or over flakes, but eventually we freed them by jumarring on them as we had done near the summit. We encountered every kind of anchor imaginable, from slung horns to multiple pieces equalized, and had a hell of a time lowering the bags. We suffered like champions. We managed to reach the ground after three days of descent. So you won't have to suffer as we did, here are some secrets on descending and rappelling to make your journey a bit easier.

PLAN AHEAD

The first defense against retreat is careful planning. Scout the weather forecast before leaving the ground. Consult the climbers topo, if one is available, for your intended route. Check to see whether there are fixed rappel anchors on the route or a designated descent route.

If you do have to retreat, self-rescue is always the best way to go. Talk through each scenario and have a plan for each rappel or lower before you are separated. It's very difficult to hear clearly on a wall, especially during a storm or in windy conditions. Create a silent communication system using hand signals or rope signals you both understand. Double-check your systems and your partner's systems before trusting anything. Divide the work evenly and work together to have a smooth-operating descent. Mistakes are made when you're tired so if you get sloppy; stop for the night and continue when you're rested.

If you can't do a self-rescue, then call for help. Once a rescue party is required, more people are at risk and it might take even longer than getting down yourself. In remote areas, self-rescue is usually the only way down because there's no one even available to make a rescue (self-rescue is discussed in Chapter 4). By preparing yourself for the worst, you're more likely to get away safely to climb another day. There's an old saying that goes "Live to wimp again." Listen to it.

RAPPEL ANCHORS

Most trade routes that see a lot of traffic have bolted anchors, which makes it easier to retreat, but don't count on them being equipped with slings. If you do use a fixed anchor, check the pieces of gear; make sure the slings are still safe and don't have burn marks or are badly faded by the sun. Before trusting a fixed anchor, always test it by clipping in to the anchor but stay backed up to the rappel, then bounce on each piece. If you question it, back it up with a new sling and/or add another piece of gear as a backup. Place a backup piece clipped in to the rappel anchor with a little slack so you fully test the anchor. If the anchor fails, then the backup saves you. If the anchor is good, the last person removes the backup piece.

If there aren't any fixed anchors, you'll have to make them. Make safe anchors and check old fixed anchors on any descent, no matter how much gear you have to leave. Lots of people have died during descents by making errors or by not making safe anchors and then having them pull. A minimum of two pieces of gear is standard, especially with heavy haul bags and the rest of the heavy gear the anchors have to hold. Equalize the pieces with a sling, webbing, or cord as you would a belay anchor, and tie a power point if possible. Add an extra piece or two as backup and remove them when the last person descends.

Always tie a knot in the end of the ropes when doing multiple rappels so you can't slide off the ends by accident.

BACKUP SYSTEMS

When rappelling long faces, it's always a good idea to use some kind of backup. There are several methods for backing up a rappel. A great way to help control speed on a rappel is by using leather gloves. Here are some other ideas.

Shunt. This is a locking device that's clamped onto the rope above the rappel device with a sling attached to your belay loop. Held in the hand and without being weighted, it slides freely over the rope, but if you lose control of the rappel or want to stop, the device locks onto the rope when weighted by you letting go with your hand. When you're ready to continue, pull down on the device with your hand to unweight it, and you're on your way.

GriGri. On a single fixed rope larger than 10 mm, you can use a GriGri as a rappel device, with the same results. When you let go with your hands, you stop. Pull

A shunt

the lever and you start down again.

Autoblock or prusik knot. Perhaps the best backup system is a prusik knot or an autoblock knot. An autoblock knot is easily released after being weighted and slides freely over the rope under your hand. It works like the Shunt but can be made with any piece of cord or sling. Here's how to make one:

1. Put either a locking or nonlocking biner on the leg loop of your brake-hand side.

Tying an autoblock knot, step 1

Tying an autoblock knot, step 2

Tying an autoblock knot, step 3

Autoblock knot engaged while rappelling

2. Girth-hitch one end of a 1- to 2-foot piece of webbing or sling (a shoulder sling works great) onto the leg loop.

3. Now wrap the remainder of the sling four or five times around both ropes and clip the end in to the biner on your leg loop. If you make too many wraps, you'll have a hard time moving down; too few, and the knot won't engage. Be sure the remaining loop of webbing is not too long because it can slide up and get caught in the rappel device.

4. When rappelling, place your brake hand above the knot to keep it loose and out of the way. If you let go of your brake hand, it will tighten and lock, stopping your descent. (You can use this same knot tied above the rappel device as a useful way for passing knots on fixed ropes. Clip it in to the belay loop instead of the leg loop for this position.)

Friction. You can create more friction to control speed on a rappel by using two locking biners with your rappel device, by wrapping the ropes once around your leg near your foot, or by squeezing the ropes between your feet as you rappel. You can also have your partner pull on the ropes from below, known as a firemans brake, as a backup or to decrease your speed of descent. Another way is to clip the rope through a biner on your leg loop, then feed it back up to another biner clipped in to the rappel biner, then back down to your brake hand. This creates a Z-looking friction system that will certainly give you more control.

RAPPELLING PAST ROOFS AND DOWN-AIDING

Some walls overhang dramatically; others have smaller roofs on vertical faces, making for exciting leads but terrifying retreats. If you have to retreat down an overhanging cliff or past large roofs, here are some tricks to make it smooth.

First of all, if you know you'll make it to the ground in a few hours or one day, dump most of your water: 1 gallon weighs more than 8 pounds. You hauled it up, but you don't need to drag it back down. If you think it might take two days or more (which is unusual), then consider keeping enough for that amount of time and dump the rest.

The first person to rappel carries the rack, including a hammer and aiders, and is ready to down-aid the roof or overhang. You can either rappel on both ropes or fix one while dragging the end of the other one with you. Set up an autoblock knot (described above) so you can use both hands to down-aid a section while on rappel. You also have the option of being lowered by your partner as you down-aid. If you do this, clip the rope through a directional on the anchor instead of belaying right off the harness. Go down to the lip of the roof, place a piece of gear, and clip the ropes in to it. Work your way down the roof by aiding across it with a pair of aiders and your daisy chains as if you were leading, clipping in the rope as you go. You are backed up by your rappel.

Once you're back on the vertical wall, resume rappelling until you need to pass another roof or reach an anchor. As you descend gently overhanging terrain, you may need to place pieces of gear to keep you against the wall rather than rappelling out into space. After you reach the next anchor and clip both ends of the ropes in to it, the second then rappels and pulls out all the gear the first person used to make it past the roof. If it's a horizontal roof, the second might have to down-aid it too, taking the pieces out on the way. It's helpful to pull down on the ropes to create more friction for the second, so gear is easier to remove. It's also helpful to offer tension from below by pulling down on the ropes to help the second swing in from space to the belay.

RAPPELLING WITH HAUL BAGS

If there are fixed anchors and the descent route is in a straight line without any roofs, traverses, or overhanging terrain, you'll make good time. Set up your rappel and decide who descends with what gear, splitting it up evenly. If you're a party of three or more, the second person down goes without any gear, if possible, because it's much easier and faster to clean the gear on rappel without being weighed down. Then the rest of the party has a clean free-hanging rappel, making it simple to rappel with haul bags. If you're a party of two, the second climber has to rap with the bags. The rest of the gear usually goes with the first person down so he or she can set up the next rappel anchor without the cumbersome bag getting in the way.

If you get the haul bag, don't wear it on your back: it will make you top heavy, and rappelling in space with it on your back certainly will turn you upside down—you'll be in a world of hurt as you hang there. Instead, girth-hitch the haul-bag straps with a shoulder sling and clip it in to your belay loop with a locking biner (see Figure 19). Use another sling as a leash for clipping it in to the rappel anchors so it's not always hanging on you while you wait for your partner. As you weight your rappel device,

PRUSIK EXTENDED FROM LEG LOOP. KEEP IT SHORT ENOUGH TO NOT INTERFERE WITH RAPPEL DEVICE.

CLIPPED TO BELAY LOOP AND HUNG BETWEEN LEGS

Figure 19. *Hang the haul bag off your rappel loop and you can rap in comfort and control.*

the bag's weight is lifted off you and onto the belay loop, making it easy to descend with the bag between your legs, where you can easily control it.

LOWERING HAUL BAGS

If you don't want to rappel with the haul bags, you can lower them from anchor to anchor. This system works only on slabs and vertical walls. Fix one rope and send down the bags on the second rope, while someone rappels the fixed rope and guides the bags down to the next belay.

On overhangs or traverses, you'll have to lower the bags without a person to guide them. You do this by clipping the bags in to a rope fixed between the two rappel anchors as a guide and then lowering the bags on the second rope. Here's how:

1. Make sure the guide rope that's fixed between the two rappel anchors is pulled taut. If it's not, the bags will hang in space away from the next anchor with no way for your partner to pull them in to the anchor. If it's taut, they will slide right into the lower anchor.
2. To lower the bags, clip them in to the second rope with a locking biner, then clip the rope through a directional on the highest point in the anchor and then to your belay device on the belay loop of your harness.
3. You can get the bags off the belay by doing a minihaul with your belay device through the directional by counterweighting them.

Autoblock engaged while rappelling with a haul bag

Rappelling with a haul bag with autoblock disengaged

4. Unclip the bags from the anchor and slowly lower them down to the next anchor.

If you have three ropes, you can do a variation on this lowering system. The first person rappels on a single rope, trailing the second rope, and fixes the first rope to the next anchor without pulling it taut as explained in step 1. The second rope is used to pull in the bags to the lower anchor as they are lowered on the third rope from above. After the gear is lowered, the second person ties the first and third ropes together and rappels on them. You can repeat this process or mix the various ways of rappelling with all the gear as the terrain dictates.

CHAPTER 3

Alex Lowe and Mark Synnott up high on the first ascent of Parallel Worlds (VII 5.11 A4), on Great Trango Tower, Pakistan

Advanced Techniques

This chapter describes the proper techniques for speed climbing, multiday climbing, first ascents, and solo climbing. Included are many shortcuts and tricks that will prove invaluable, whether you want to climb faster or simply alone.

SPEED CLIMBING

Speed climbing has taken a firm stance in the modern arsenal of climbing styles. Besides allowing climbers to get up routes faster, it's safer. The less time you spend on a cliff, the more you're out of potential danger. Speed climbing is a survival tool on alpine and remote walls where escaping a harsh storm could save your life. It's also really fun to look back at a route and know you did it fast, boosting your confidence and your experience.

To climb faster, you need to know all the jumar and belay systems, all the transition and management skills discussed in Chapter 2, Basic Wall-Climbing Procedures. You need to read the placements quickly and feel confident with your gear. And you need tons of practice.

This section introduces methods for efficiently leading in blocks or "leapfrogging" leads and short-fixing the rope. These multipitch free-climbing techniques will help you avoid stressful situations, for a more efficient climbing experience whether you're speed climbing or not. Get these systems dialed for more time to be with your surroundings and connect with the wall climbing experience.

LEADING IN BLOCKS
One of the fastest ways to climb pitches quickly is to lead in blocks. Leading in blocks means that one person leads a number of consecutive pitches while the

second climber jumars (fastest) or free climbs to clean the pitch. Here are several reasons why this is effective:

- There is no need to exchange the entire rack at each belay.
- While the second is jumarring or climbing, the leader can rest, drink, eat, and get prepared for the next lead.
- The second can jumar a pitch much faster than climbing it.
- The leader gets into lead mode and stays there till his or her block is finished, usually several pitches in length.

This system of leading in blocks has led to extremely fast ascents of big walls from Yosemite to the Himalaya. However, it can be applied to any wall situation. Leading in blocks runs in this order:

1. The leader climbs a pitch and gives the belayer a 5-minute or less warning that he or she is almost at the anchor.

KEY EXERCISE: PRACTICING AT A CRAG

Practice at the crag and test yourself on how fast and efficient you can perform these skills. Pick a route that's three to five pitches long and see how fast you can climb it safely, starting on easy to moderate aid with a mix of free climbing. Change the climbing terrain from slabs to overhangs so you master them all, and talk with your partner about how things could be done more efficiently to develop a rhythm that keeps you moving fast but not so fast as to be unsafe. By testing your skills on the small crags, you'll know how the whole system works when you're on the big stone.

2. After this warning, the belayer gets ready to follow by tying shoes, disassembling part of the anchor (always have two solid pieces left), racking gear, getting the bags ready to haul, or shouldering a pack.

3. The leader calls out "Off belay" and "Rope fixed" or "On belay" to let the second climber know he or she can take the belay off and start to move.

4. The leader hauls the bag while the second is jumarring or climbing.

5. The second gets to the anchor and clips the gear to the leader's rack while the leader starts placing the first piece of gear on the next pitch.

6. Repeat steps 1–5 to the end of the block.

For this system to work, the leader and belayer have to perform specific jobs, as follows. The leader will:

1. At the end of the pitch, set up the anchor and get off belay as soon as possible.

2. Pull up the slack in the rope and fix it for the second to jumar on, or put the second on belay as soon as possible.

3. Set up the haul and get the bag off the lower belay so the second can start moving.

4. Haul and belay at the same time if the second doesn't jumar.

5. After hauling, set up the bag with the rope stacked so it's ready to go for the next pitch before the second arrives.

6. Place the first piece of gear on the next pitch.

7. Organize the gear and ropes for the next lead.

8. Drink, eat, and rest.

The belayer/second will:

1. During a lead, call out "Halfway" to let the leader know how much rope is left; for example, "You have twenty-five feet left."

2. Have the haul bag packed and ready to go before the leader gets to the end of the pitch.

3. Remove extra pieces in the anchor and break down anything else just before the lead is finished.

4. Have shoes and/or jumars ready to go before the leader fixes or belays.

5. Rack the gear neatly while cleaning, for easy passing to the leader at the belay.

6. Arrive at the anchor and immediately put the leader on belay, pass gear, and stack the lead rope while hanging on the jumars. Once the leader is leading and off the anchor, clip directly in to the anchor and remove the jumars and knots from the lead rope.

7. Belay; eat, drink, and rest while belaying.

Some important tools for these jobs include:

- GriGri, Reverso, Cinch, or any locking belay device
- Mini Traxion or similar hauling device
- Jumars, etriers, and cleaning tools (funkness device, nut tool)

These tools provide safety while you're

multitasking and make these systems work faster. You can use a regular pulley and jumar for hauling and a nonlocking belay device for belaying, but your hands won't be available for other tasks.

Deciding how many pitches to lead in a block depends on the route and the strengths of the climbers. Let's say a climber leads four pitches in a row, which lead to a ledge. Stop at the ledge and change over the lead there. Having a ledge makes transitions easier because you can stand and stack ropes, etc. If several pitches of aid are followed by a few of free climbing, split up the pitches so the stronger climber in each field is leading. Adjust the amount of pitches in a block as you go: if the leader needs a break, change over the lead. Leading duties should be shared evenly, so if one person leads for 4 hours or four pitches, so should the second.

THREE-CLIMBER LEAPFROGGING

Leapfrogging refers to a system that a party of three utilizes to make fast upward progress when aid climbing. When free climbing, leapfrogging means the second climber, who just followed the last pitch, leads the next pitch, and so forth. Here is how it works:

1. The leader climbs a pitch, fixes the lead rope, and sets up a haul on a haul rope.
2. The leader hauls the bag off the lower anchor just enough to unweight the bags from the anchor.

3. Before the leader hauls the bag, the third climber jumars the haul rope to the leader, with any extra gear and another lead rope. It's very important to back up the haul line under the hauling device because a person is jumarring up it. If there's no haul bag, the third climber jugs the second rope without a bag attached.
4. The third climber immediately puts the leader on belay on the lead rope he or she brought up and starts to haul while the second climber cleans the last pitch.
5. The third climber feeds out slack from the haul line as he or she hauls up the bag so the leader can continue.
6. The second climber reaches the anchor, and the second and third climbers organize the gear and send it up to the leader on the haul rope.
7. The leader uses the remainder of the slack left in the haul line that's up with him or her to pull up the gear and the pulley from the last pitch after the second arrives.
8. Repeat steps 1–7.

This system can be modified so the third climber starts leading on the third rope he or she brought up with him or her instead of the leader continuing in a block of pitches. However, if you have only two ropes, you won't be able to do this the same way. The system below is best suited for speed ascents. Here's what to do if you have three climbers and two ropes:

1. The third climber jumars up the haul

line and puts the leader on belay on that rope (only if there is no hauling). The haul line must be dynamic.

2. To retrieve gear from the last pitch, the leader, hanging from a solid placement, lowers down a loop of rope on the lead line to pull up the end of the second rope and the gear cleaned from the last pitch.

You don't have to be speed climbing to use these systems. They also show you how to be more efficient even if you're climbing only a few pitches a day.

SHORT-FIXING THE ROPE

Short fixing has become the primary way speed-climbing records in Yosemite have been set and broken. For instance, in 2002, Hans Florine and Yuji Hirayama climbed the Nose in 2 hours, 48 minutes by using the short-fixing system in their arsenal of tools. Most parties climb this route in two to four days! Short fixing should be reserved only for a team of two on a speed ascent when no bags are being hauled. The idea is to keep the climbers moving at all times: the leader can short-fix the rope and continue leading while the second cleans. Here's how it works:

1. After reaching the belay, the leader pulls up all the slack left in the rope and fixes it for the second to jumar on.

2. The leader continues climbing using a self-belay system (Silent Partner, etc.; see Solo Climbing later in this chapter) on the slack he or she pulled up.

3. The leader must place a piece of gear right off the belay when self-belaying to avoid falling directly onto the anchor that the second is jumarring on.

4. As soon as the second climber arrives at the belay, he or she clips directly in to the anchor, puts the leader on a regular belay, and frees the fixed line so the leader can continue climbing uninterrupted.

5. At this point, the leader uses a tag line or lowers a loop to pull up the gear cleaned from the previous pitch and then keeps moving.

As with any self-belaying practice, check your system twice before leaving the anchor, and always climb in control. Even if you make only 20 feet of progress in the time it takes the second to clean the pitch, it's still better than not making any upward progress at all.

MULTIDAY CLIMBS

Multiday wall climbs that involve porta-ledge bivies with big exposure and require you to haul gear, food, and water are a big deal. Many climbers talk for a long time about doing a multiday big wall climb, but actually packing up the bags and hiking to the base takes a lot of courage. Each step of the way is a journey in itself, and this is part of the process. Getting ready for a multiday wall requires planning, vision, and determination. This section describes how to prepare properly for such a climb, sparing you hours or even days of anxiety over how and what to do to get ready.

PLANNING

The length of the climb, its grade, and its difficulty all dictate approximately how long you must plan to be on it. Choose how long you want to be on the wall, from two to 10 days, according to the speed at which you like to climb. For instance, some climbers take months to climb a route in Yosemite, whereas most climbers start and finish in the same week. If you like to be up there for a long time, plan accordingly. Whatever your speed, plan for it in relation to the climb. If, for example, you plan on climbing the Nose on El Capitan and don't have too much experience, plan on a four- to six-day ascent. More-experienced parties usually do the Nose in three.

Know how hard you can climb and gauge how long it takes you on average to climb at your top level: use this to gauge how many pitches you can climb at that pace in one day. Understand that toward the end of the climb, the last day or two, you'll be worn down, probably dehydrated, and anxious to get off, so factor in more time to get started at the beginning of each day on the wall. Your hands, feet, and muscles will be sore and swollen, making it harder to get going with each day that goes by, and this adds to the difficulty of any climb. Add to the equation the tasks of hauling and cleaning and the endless job of pulling up ropes, and the difficulty grows in far more ways than a simple number can indicate.

The harder the climbing, the slower you'll go. Fear is debilitating and slows climbing down considerably. Getting everything organized, eating and drinking, plus racking and breaking down camp every morning takes longer for the inexperienced climber.

One of the most important considerations in planning the time you'll need on a wall is weather. It has caused so many failures, and even deaths, that it must be taken seriously. Don't go up on a big climb if you know it's going to storm. Wait it out. If it looks good for three days with a chance of rain on the fourth day, but you need at least four days to do the climb, shuffle around the days so you miss the storm.

Once you've gauged how fast you climb against how hard the route is rated and the overall grade, you'll have a good idea of how many days to plan for. Always plan for at least an extra day because stretched food

KEY EXERCISE: GAUGING YOUR CLIMBING PACE

To judge how fast you go, aid a few pitches at your local crag and then add on an hour per pitch for hauling plus a little more to compensate for inefficiency, fear, and weather, and use this as a time meter. This will give you a rough idea of how fast you climb.

and water supplies can catch you in a tight spot. If you think your skills are solid for a three-day ascent, add a day or two of food and water in case of bad weather or other possible delays.

PORTALEDGES

One of the greatest parts of climbing a big wall is living out of a portaledge up high on the cliff. Portaledges were first introduced in the late '70s for wall climbing in Yosemite National Park and beyond, in alpine arenas. They have evolved from Warren Harding's hammocks into refined ledge systems that are comfortable, safe, and reliable. To make sure you have a good experience, you need a solid portaledge that will stand up to a harsh storm and that includes a dependable storm fly. Reliable shelter is your best bet for having a fun wall experience but, more important, it is also your best defense against hypothermia, which could require a rescue. I've survived some of the worst weather imaginable at 20,000 feet in the Himalayas in a portaledge by making sure every seam was sealed and in working order long before I set foot on the wall.

A portaledge is constructed from a nylon bed that's supported by collapsible aluminum tubing suspended by six adjustable straps. The nylon bed is kept taut by the adjustable straps attached to the tubing. The single clip-in point makes it simple to move and set up. It looks like a suspended cot you would use when camping. The rain fly covers the ledge similarly to a tent, with a cinch cord and buckled straps to keep it in place should any wind occur. It also has a single clip-in point.

Purpose. Before buying a portaledge, ask yourself what you'll use it for. Will you be doing more solo climbing or climbing mostly with a partner? Will you be setting it up only at night, or do you plan to use it as a large belay ledge during the day? Will you be doing one route a year or several? Will they be in Yosemite, Zion, or remote Baffin Island? To choose the right ledge for your needs, answer these questions first, then shop around for what will best suit your needs. If you're going to set up the portaledge at the belay, consider one that sets up fast, especially if you're planning on doing only a few routes a year (also see Belay Seats in Chapter 1, Wall Climbing Fundamentals). If you plan on solo climbing a lot, you could choose a single, but the added weight of a double is worth it for greater comfort and space.

Price. Portaledges aren't cheap. The average portaledge and rain fly costs somewhere between $475 and $700. The more you spend, the higher quality and better performing the ledge system will be. Most manufacturers sell the ledges and flies separately and offer several different styles of fly.

Rain fly. The most basic style is a single-sheet fly that covers the portaledge, has a drawstring to secure it under the ledge, and has one or two buckled straps to keep it from flapping in windy conditions. This is a good all-around system that works great for most outings; it comes in either Gore-Tex or coated nylon. I used this fly system while climbing a new route on Roraima Tepui in the rain forests of Guyana, where it rains heavily every day. It performed perfectly and kept us and all our gear dry.

A more durable, storm-proof fly is one that encloses the entire portaledge. These require that you slide the ledge inside it for full protection from storms. These models are usually made of the same materials as described above and usually have one or two doors for access; some even have a clearish window or vent hole. Two doors are better than one, especially if you have two ledges set up side by side and you want to pass things back and forth or if you set up a ledge in a dihedral and can access the ledge from only one side. If you plan on climbing mostly in Yosemite or Zion and other national parks in the United States, you can probably get by with a standard rain fly; if you plan on doing a remote wall, invest in a storm fly that encloses the entire ledge and has at least one door.

Using a rain fly with a portaledge can be cumbersome and somewhat complicated, but some flies have features for easy deployment and adjustment that make them a little easier to use. Be sure the fly has full seam taping as well as reinforced corners and a scuff guard on the bed's wall side of the fly, where it will be subject to high abrasion. In addition to getting a fly with seam-taped seams, seam-seal the outside of all seams. Some flies are built with "RF (radio-frequency)-welded" clip-in points, a durable waterproof connection borrowed from rafting technology that's easy to use. One thing to consider is getting a white or yellow fly, which creates a lighter atmosphere inside; a dark color can start to feel confining and gloomy and makes it more difficult to see inside the ledge during the day.

Almost every fly is equipped with a removable aluminum tent pole that creates more space in a portaledge by pushing out the fly for greater living space while also

KEY EXERCISE: SETTING UP THE PORTALEDGE

Before you head up on your route, spend an hour setting up and breaking down the ledge a few times to get the hang of it. Try setting up the ledge while hanging in your harness at a rock gym, on a boulder, or at a crag to simulate what you'll be doing on the wall. It's a lot harder hanging from the wall than you might think, and if it's starting to storm you'll be happy you can do it quickly. Make sure all the tube fittings work smoothly on both setup and breakdown and that the tension straps adjust easily while you're lying in the bed. It's a hassle to unweight the bed for each adjustment, especially if you're lying down.

keeping the fly material away from your sleeping bags and gear. If you plan on cooking with a hanging stove, make sure there's a daisy chain or another kind of loop hanging down from the clip-in point to accommodate it. Some flies also come with other clip-in points for managing stuff sacks and gear inside the ledge; you can also buy organizers that clip in to the suspension straps for clutter-free ledge living. Another nice feature is a mesh organizer pocket built into the separation straps in the middle of the ledge for small items that easily get lost.

Weight. Portaledges, which usually weigh 10–15 pounds, aren't light; with a fly weighing 3–5 pounds, the total is about 13–18 pounds. If you're hauling a bunch of wall gear, trying to cut back on a few pounds by using a lightweight ledge isn't wise unless you're doing long approaches or are far from home and need to cut every ounce. Your portaledge is worth its weight in gold once you're set up in it at the end of a long day and especially if you get pinned down in a storm.

Durability. Your portaledge is your home away from home, and the last thing you need is for it to fall apart while you're on your climbing route. Make sure the bed material is tear-proof and made of durable materials such as rip-stop nylon or cordura. Also look for strong aluminum tubes; solid, easily adjustable aluminum or steel buckles; and a reinforced clip-in point that can easily be clipped in to. Make sure there's reinforcement material on the wall side of the bed and that the bungee cords on the insides of the tubes are thick-gauge.

Setup and adjustment. At the end of a long day, you want to be able to set up your ledge quickly without frustrations. Setting one up while you are hanging in your harness is difficult, but most ledges can be set up within 10 minutes or less after you've had some practice.

Some ledges have bed tension straps to get the bed drum tight, a feature you'll appreciate if the material stretches over time or is wet from a storm. A colored clip-in point is handy when you unpack the ledge out of its haul bag for easy clipping to the anchor. Always pack the ledge away in its haul bag with the clip-in point readily available for the next time you need to set it up, and always try to pack it up clean and neat without the straps getting too tangled, which can make for a frustrating cluster later on.

Size. There are two basic styles of ledges: single and double. They all vary in length, so if you're tall, go big because this will be the only horizontal "ground" on the route, and sleeping with your head or feet resting on the end tubes is no fun. Whether to use a larger one or a smaller one is a trade-off because each has its own value. The larger ones offer more room for waiting out storms, cooking and sleeping, racking, and just hanging out, but they are heavier than the smaller ones. Some double ledges hang one single ledge under the other. There is also a three-person ledge that is made of a double ledge with a hammock that hangs under it; the hammock is removable for two-person climbs, adding more versatility.

As a belay seat. I usually use a porta-ledge as the ultimate power-lounge belay

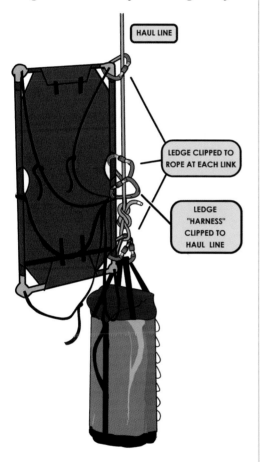

HAUL LINE

LEDGE CLIPPED TO ROPE AT EACH LINK

LEDGE "HARNESS" CLIPPED TO HAUL LINE

Figure 20. *Hauling an open portaledge: the ledge can spin freely in the wind and is easy to set up at the next anchor for the ultimate belay seat.*

seat by hauling it while it's set up, which is very easy and worthwhile. It works only when you're hauling on very steep to overhanging terrain, because otherwise it can snag on the face and get damaged. The best way is to clip it in to the haul line with two locking biners in a vertical position, like a sail (see Figure 20). Clip in two corners of the ledge to the line and the suspension straps, and it will spin around on the line in the wind. You can also haul it from the ledge's main clip-in point, but then it could really snag or spin as you haul.

ADDITIONAL GEAR

In addition to the gear listed in Chapter 1, Wall-Climbing Fundamentals, bring a sleeping bag and a pad, unless you're someplace where it's always hot and sunny. A closed-cell foam pad that's about $3/8$–$1/2$ inch thick is ideal because the thicker ones are heavier and take up too much room in the haul bag. Never bring an air mattress, for obvious reasons. Make a leash for the pad by duct-taping both sides of a corner about 3 inches deep, then poke a hole in it, and make a clip-in loop with some string. I've lost pads in the wind and from stupid-ity. The main reasons to bring the pad are to protect the load in the haul bag and to keep you warmer at night. I've gone without a pad, and it was unpleasant, to say the least. Get a good synthetic sleeping bag that is suited to the lowest temperatures you plan to encounter. Bringing a lighter bag can work if you have a good parka to wear inside it, but if it all gets wet, you'll be in trouble. Down bags compress smaller and have greater fill while being lighter than synthetics, but they are as worthless as a limp dishrag when they're wet.

A bivy sack is a really good idea if you want foolproof protection from any weather, especially considering that during a storm the inside of a fly condenses and drips on you. A fully sealed Gore-Tex bivy sack used with a sleeping bag, pad, and rain fly will get you through the worst that nature can throw at you. Features to look for in a good bivy sack include seam-taped construction, 100 percent Gore-Tex material (not half coated nylon), a two-way zippered shoulder-height entry with storm flaps, and a tie-in tunnel. Some bivy sacks now have RF-welded seams incorporated into the tie-in point for a completely waterproof seal.

Additional personal items to increase comfort at the bivy include a toothbrush, toothpaste, and towelettes or baby wipes (for washing your face, hands, and privates after going to the bathroom). Some people like to bring a small radio or speakers that plug into an MP3 player. A book can help relieve hours of boredom while belaying or sitting out a storm, and a pen comes in handy for drawing a chess board or checker board or for writing. Once I had a partner who brought a men's magazine up a wall; he stuffed a naughty picture in a crack at every belay to torture the next party.

SETTING UP A BIVY

Finding the perfect bivy site is almost impossible. Things to look for are shelter from wind and rain (roofs), a spacious ledge you can walk around on, good cracks or spread-out anchors to keep things in order, and a clean vertical wall that your portaledge will rest against evenly. Avoid slabs, corners, arêtes, or potential drainages in case of bad weather because setting up your ledges and gear is more difficult in these cases. Avoid having to set up a bivy in cramped areas or where there's only a small vertical crack: hanging everything from one point in a corner is very frustrating. If you're using two single portaledges, ideally you want to hang them next to but not able to touch each other, with the haul bags within reach. If you have to set up two ledges—singles or doubles—vertically, set them up on a length of rope coming off the main anchor stacked on top of each other.

Once you've made it to the bivy site, and hopefully you've made it before dark, set things up for the night. If it's already dark, you'll have your headlamps on already (keep them at the top of the haul bag for easy access). Set up the portaledge(s) with the fly ready to deploy, adjust it to hang evenly horizontal, and sit down for a second. Nice, huh? Have your partner start handing you things from the haul bag, starting with the sleeping pads, then the sleeping bags, then food, water, and personal gear. At the bivy you'll need a lot of spare biners to clip food and personal stuff sacks to the portaledge. I've lost a lot of things in this process.

Do all your cooking and eating with the portaledge's middle suspension fins down and one person on either end of the ledge, with your backs against the wall for maximum comfort. If you are using two single ledges, you can share one while cooking and eating or lounge on your own. Clip the food bags, water, and cooking gear to one of the middle ledge straps so you can get to them easily. Now stuff your face and relax. If you use a hanging stove, clip it to the middle suspension strap so it hangs away from all the straps and is high enough above the bed not to melt it. When using a hanging stove, monitor it closely and try not to move the portaledge much because these stoves swing easily and can dump your dinner quickly. Yeah, I've made just about every mistake you can with these. A pair of pot grips is a lifesaver.

Once you're wedged, take the food and other gear and either stuff it back in the haul bag or, better yet, clip it to the clip-in point for the portaledge at the top of the suspension harness. This keeps it close at hand while not taking up bed space; if you have the fly down, it will keep everything dry and prevent you from having to go out in a storm to get the things. In good weather, you can also clip stuff sacks to a strap and let them hang below the portaledge.

ROPE MANAGEMENT

On a longer climb, it's a chore to constantly manage the rope or ropes you're climbing with. Yet if you don't handle the ropes properly, you'll waste time dealing with tangled ropes and possible snags. To eliminate these pesky problems, follow these guidelines:

- Once you've tied in to the anchor, clip the rope leading down to the second through a free biner or quickdraw clipped in to a piece above you in the anchor. This allows you to pull down on the rope instead of up when belaying the second climber. It also will pull you into the belay instead of down on your harness if the second falls, and it creates a perfect place for the second to hang on a clove hitch when he or she arrives at the belay. It acts as a redirection so you can easily stack the rope across your lap as you pull it in.

- Tying in to the anchor with your end of the rope creates a perfect place to stack the rope. If you use twin ropes, stack them both at the same time across your lap. If you use a single rope and a tag line, pull up the tag line first and stack it either in a sling, in an overhand tied with a large loop, or on a ledge, then set up the second rope and stack it across your lap.

- A tag line, if stacked well, will simply feed out without any attention so you can concentrate on the belay.

- Never let a rope hang in a huge loop below the belay! It can snag in cracks, catch on knobs, or be blown around a corner in the wind.

- If you need to pull up a rope and stack it, clip it in to a directional above you so you can pull it down and stack it instead of having to pull up.

FIXING ROPES

Fixing ropes is a common practice while wall climbing, and there are different situations in which you would fix them. The most common is when you've climbed the first two or three pitches of a route and you plan to sleep on the ground before blasting off up the wall in the near future. Here's how to do the anchor point–to–anchor point method:

1. Fix your haul line (usually a static rope) and lead rope or ropes to the high-point anchor, just as you would if you were leading a pitch.
2. Rappel to the next anchor below and fix the rope in to it in the same manner as above.
3. At each anchor, leave at least 5 feet of slack in the rope so the next person has enough slack to rappel. If you fix the rope in tight to the anchor, it's nearly impossible for the next person to rappel the line.
4. Repeat steps 1–3 till you reach the ground. Fix the bottom end of the rope to the ground too to keep the wind from snagging it up the wall or in a tree. If there is extra rope left over at a belay, coil it up to prevent it from snagging.

Another situation in which you would fix ropes occurs while you're on the wall. Let's say you've climbed four pitches and think you might have enough time for one or two more, but not if you include the hauling. In this case, it's best to lead a pitch or two and fix the ropes in place for the following day, and then return to your bags and portaledge for the night. This is especially true if you have a nice, spacious natural ledge that makes a perfect bivy and you don't want to have a hanging bivy.

While one person climbs, the second can start setting up the ledge, etc. If this is the case, the second climber cleans the pitch and leaves the gear at the top of the pitch, but the leader could also fix the haul line and rappel or simply clean the pitch on rappel. It's better to leave the gear up on the pitch so you don't have to jumar with it later. Below are some tips for fixing ropes.

Protect the rope. The number-one thing to do when fixing ropes is to make sure the rope doesn't run across any sharp edges that could potentially cut or saw through the rope. Tape any sharp edges with athletic tape or duct tape for safety. Remove it when you're done. Place a directional to keep ropes away from cracks and edges. Use a wrap-around rope protector if necessary. You can also wrap a sling or a prusik around the rope, using tape to keep it in place, to protect the rope from a bad edge or friction zone. If the rope's sheath gets worn, move the rope away or pull it up and fix it shorter to avoid it rubbing in the same place. When jumarring any fixed rope, never bounce on the rope; it can cut through on even dull edges or on a burr on a piton. I watched my partner jumar a rope on Nameless Tower, and the bouncing action caused the rope to cut through and explode into two pieces. Just moments before the rope snapped, we had thrown down another rope that he had clipped in to. It saved his life!

Save slings and cordelettes. Use an equalized figure eight: begin as normal for a figure eight on a bight, but don't pull the final loop through all the way. Pull the end loop over the knot and cinch it tight below the main bight. Equalize the upper loops to the proper lengths and when the knot is weighted, it will snug tight.

Wet ropes. If your ropes are wet, leave a lot of slack when fixing them because ropes shrink as they dry. I've had a fixed rope shrink so much that it pulled up and out on a piece of gear in the lower anchor, making it dangerous and unsafe. The rope stretches when rappelling and jumarring too, so always leave some slack in the system when fixing.

Wind. Don't fix the rope too tight because wind can whip the rope back and forth across sharp edges that will saw through it. However, don't fix the rope too loose because the wind can whip it off to the side and it could catch on a flake, making it impossible to retrieve.

Overhangs. If you plan on fixing the first few pitches but they're overhanging, rather than fixing anchor to anchor you can tie two or more ropes together with a figure eight follow-through till it reaches the ground. You'll have to pass knots on the way down and up, but it's easier than lowering out from or rappelling into each anchor point. Another advantage is that you can reach a longer distance by tying them together because most pitches are less than 200 feet.

The disadvantage is that you have to wait till each climber is all the way up or down before you can go, and the rope stretch and "bounce" effect is pronounced near the bottom of a long string of fixed rope.

On overhanging terrain, the climber cleaning the pitches to be fixed has to fix the bottom end of the rope to the anchor before starting to clean the pitch, and then this climber won't be able to tie a backup knot while cleaning the pitch. If you don't fix the rope before you clean, you'll have to down-aid the overhanging terrain in order to get back to the anchor. On Great Trango Tower in Pakistan, I left two ropes fixed on an extremely overhanging section of the climb to facilitate our descent. Without them, it would have been nearly impossible to down-climb the horizontal seam, and we would have been left hanging more than 50 feet out in space. Leave enough slack in the fixed line on a steep roof so the rope hangs in an arch. This makes jumarring and rappelling easier than if the rope is tight. Fix the rope on an overhang with a short knot tied in to the anchor so when you jumar up to the anchor, your jumars don't stop a few feet below the anchor. It's a hassle to have to climb up to the anchor on this terrain.

SAFETY-CHECKING FIXED ROPES BEFORE CLIMBING

Climbing fixed ropes can be more dangerous than lead climbing because you are totally relying on the rope being safe. The rope could be damaged if there was rockfall during the night, strong winds that whipped your rope back and forth across the face, or a freeze-thaw cycle that changed the strength of the anchor. From below, you'll have no idea whether the rope is safe to climb. Before jumping on a fixed rope, use this safety checklist:

- Always do a visual inspection of the rope from anchor to anchor to your best ability before committing to it. If you see a fray in the rope or if the rope is stuck behind a flake, make sure it's safe or free it first.

- Don't jumar up a rope that's stuck behind a flake off to the side because your weight could pry the flake off and it could fall down onto you. The bouncing action on a rope stuck behind a flake can also cause it to saw through without you being able to see it.

- Pay attention to the rope: check for wear and tear and if it's getting worn out in one area, protect it or move it. If there is a section of sheath missing, don't use the rope.

- If you don't trust the fixed rope, don't use it. Relead the pitch. An alternative is to jumar the rope while on belay with another rope, placing protection as you go in case the fixed rope breaks.

TRANSITIONS ON FIXED ROPES

When you're jumarring more than one fixed rope, you'll have to pass knots and/or anchors. Follow these procedures to make transitions easy and efficient. Always check anchors, locking biners, and your system before you unclip from an anchor and start another jumarring section.

Passing a knot. Tie ropes together using a figure eight follow-through, leaving a 4-foot tail on one of the ropes. Tie either an overhand or a figure eight on a bight on the tail. This is to clip in to with a daisy chain or spare sling as you pass one jumar at a time past the knot. Unclip it as you continue up. It's just a backup as you pass the jumars past the knot.

Passing an anchor. When you arrive at an anchor with another rope fixed above, clip in to the anchor point with another daisy chain or sling, grab the next rope, and pass one jumar at a time onto it. Take the stretch out of the next rope by using your jumars to pull the rope tight, unclip from the anchor, and continue up.

Passing an overhang. On overhanging fixed ropes, you'll have to lower yourself out. First, use both jumars to pull the rope tight, allowing the top jumar to take your weight. Next, using the slack in the rope, use either a rappel device or a Münter hitch on a biner attached to your belay loop to lower yourself out. You're basically rappelling off the anchor to let yourself out from the wall. Unclip yourself from the anchor and slowly lower yourself out, letting all your weight go onto the jumars. If it's a long way out, keep jumarring as you lower yourself out, unless you have enough slack in the rope to lower all the way out so you're hanging directly under the next anchor. This is somewhat intimidating, but the exposure on a big roof is one of the best parts of a big wall, so take a deep breath and enjoy it.

Passing a traverse. If your ropes are fixed on a traverse, you'll have to rap down the rope to the low point between the two anchors first, then clip on your jumars and jumar up to the next anchor. Clip a biner through the top hole of the jumars, where the cam attaches to the rope, to keep it from potentially popping off the rope on the traverse.

RAPPELLING FIXED ROPES

When you rappel fixed ropes, especially on smaller-diameter ropes, you're rappelling a single rope that's more difficult to control. To increase friction and control, use two biners on the stitch plate–type belay device to increase friction and an autoblock to be safe. You can use a GriGri on fixed ropes, but it takes a lot of practice to get used to. Gloves are strongly recommended in any rappelling situation. If that's not enough, clip a biner to your leg loop, run the rope through it, then redirect the rope through another biner clipped in to your rappel-device biner to create a "Z" drag. You can also wrap the rope around your leg. Always check anchors, locking biners, and your system before you unclip from an anchor and start another rappel.

Untangling the rope. When fixed ropes get a lot of travel, they tend to get kinks and tangles in them from running through the devices with both ends fixed. If the rope gets a lot of kinks in it, remove the rope from the anchor and let the kinks spin out, then refix it. Of course, you have to let your partner know this before he or she is on the rope. The more you rappel on a rope, the more kinks it'll get, so do this often if it's bad.

Passing a knot. On rappel, leave about 8 inches of slack before the knot comes tight to the device and, using your jumars, hang on the rope. Remove the rappel device, pull up the rope below the knot, and set up your rappel device so it's tight against the bottom of the knot. Clip an aider in to the lower jumar, step up, switch your weight to the rappel device, and remove the jumars. Repeat these steps on your way down. If you don't have jumars, use prusiks.

Rappelling an overhang. On big overhangs, you'll have to rappel down to the low point in the rope before you can pull yourself in to the anchor. This will be lower than the anchor you're going to. At this point, attach your jumars and ascend to the anchor, allowing the rappel device to lower you in to the wall. Clip in to the anchor, transfer to the next rope, and continue on. If the rope is too tight or too loose, adjust it properly for the next person for efficiency. Remember, you're a team, so work for each other and together.

FIRST ASCENTS

A big wall first ascent is something you build up to. It's a reflection of who you are, what you believe in, what climbing style you practice, your boldness, and your talent and ability to envision and complete a climb. It can be a hundred feet or thousands of feet long, depending on what you want to do and where you plan to climb. There's so much out there yet undiscovered that you could do a first ascent every time you climb if you have the desire and skill to do it. When I started climbing, I wanted to do first ascents even though I didn't have a clue about what they entailed—but the passion was there. I read so many books about climbing, from the Himalayan giants to the classics in Yosemite, and was always intrigued by those who led the way that they seemed to shape my destiny without my really knowing it.

First ascents involve ethics, climbing style, efficiency, vision, talent, and determination. Knowing where you stand regarding these aspects is paramount. To gain knowledge of these, climb a lot of various routes in different styles so you know which one's for you. Gain experience in each field before trying to do a first ascent. By doing so, you see what others have done and learn what might be possible for yourself. If you simply go and start drilling bolts where an experienced climber wouldn't have, you're falling short of the climbing community's standards and simply scarring and destroying the rock. Similarly, if you start up a new route on a big alpine peak and get nailed by a serac avalanche, you probably didn't know that you were in one of the most dangerous places to climb on a peak. Learning the necessary skills, knowing the history of

each style, knowing the ethics of those who came before you, and applying your talent make for grand achievements in climbing.

After a few years of climbing, I turned my eyes away from the established routes and started to see my own. I had learned the skills, sharpened my vision of what I wanted to do, found where I could do it, and commenced to make it happen. You too can make your dream climb come true if you apply the proper knowledge and skills. Climbing is fun but dangerous, and first ascents are even more so. Using good judgment is the first priority when it comes to first ascents, and attaining good judgment takes time. All the skills in this book are mandatory for a big wall first ascent; however, simply reading about them and learning them don't mean you're ready to do a first ascent.

On a first ascent, you make the decisions on everything: routefinding, length of pitches, how hard or how safe you're going to make it, and where and when to drill bolts. When you repeat a route, you have a map showing you where to go, what gear you need, the difficulty, and the dangers; the fact that it's been done means it goes all the way to the top. First ascents are in a totally different league. You can be bold or you can be a wimp. Completing a first ascent that you're proud of requires a lot of past experience that you draw on as you make crucial decisions along the way. If you come up to a long section of hooking or an expanding flake on a first ascent, you decide right then how hard and dangerous you're going to make it.

One ethical debate revolves around whether to drill bolts to make a route safe. Ask yourself whether someone in the future would do the route without bolts, and if so, whether you should continue without them or retreat and leave it for a party who can do the climb without bolts. Less is always more, and it's better to leave it for someone in the future who can do it without compromising the purity of the route. Of course, climbing is total anarchy and you can do whatever you want. There are no rules. But ultimately you'll have to live with your decisions and be accountable for them. By gaining experience and following the local code of ethics, you learn to make the right decisions about boldness.

PLANNING

When planning a first ascent, you need a solid plan of attack and retreat, a calculated number of days, the corresponding amount of food and water required, the necessary hardware and ropes, descent options, clothing and bivy gear, as well as routefinding options. First you need to decide on the route and plan your style of ascent accordingly. The intended route will dictate how to plan for it.

Alpine style or single push. This is usually applied to a route that can be done quickly. Because you carry all the gear on your back and can cover more ground in a day than on a wall, alpine style demands a lighter amount of food and usually a source of water that can be found on the route (ice, snow, or drips).

Capsule style. This is applied to a route that takes more time and requires you to haul gear instead of carrying it on your back. Because you'll be hauling more gear and climbing slower on a more technically demanding route with aid climbing, capsule style demands more food and water.

You can integrate both styles into one ascent. If your intended route has a long alpinelike approach before a wall or if there is an alpine finish to a wall, you apply one style of climbing to each of these sections as needed: for instance, a capsule-style climb with an alpine-style finish. Choose the route and the style, decide how many days you need, and then decide what kind of food and gear you'll need.

Food and water. Either style requires enough food and water for the number of days planned, plus a few for bad weather. If you fail to complete your new route because you didn't have enough food or water, you're not only going to be really bummed, but you'll have to go back and try it again. This isn't always an option. If I had failed on Shipton Spire in Pakistan, I would never have had another shot at it that year: if we had had to rappel, we would've left the rack behind on rappel anchors, which would have left us with nothing to climb with for another attempt. As it was, we had to stretch 10 days of food to 15, and we barely made it through a week of continuous bad weather to the top. Plan your food so you can stretch it out during bad weather and still make it.

Climbing gear. After scoping the line with a spotting scope or binoculars and drawing a sketch of it, decide what hardware you need. If you don't see any really wide cracks, you can leave behind the heavy, wide cams and gear. If you think some features will blank out, requiring you to drill a rivet ladder, bring enough of them, or use removable bolts to cut back on weight. If you think it's going to be mostly free climbing, you can trim back on or not bring any pitons or other aid climbing gear at all. The idea is to trim or add to the rack according to what you think you'll need so you're prepared for anything you encounter. A triple set of camming devices from very small to 4 inches, a set of RPs and stoppers, 12 runners, 8 quickdraws, 25–50 nonlocking carabiners, and a selection of pitons, hooks, copper heads, and anything else you think you might want will pretty much get you up anything. A small hand-drill bolt kit, complete with spare bits and all the hardware you think you'll need, is required if you plan on drilling.

Descent. You need to plan for your descent too. If you plan to rappel the route, make sure you can get down roofs and traverses without too much trouble. Retreating or rappelling in a storm is unpleasant. Be sure you'll have enough gear and slings to make it all the way down. If it's too complicated or time-consuming to rappel, walk off. Scout the descent beforehand so you don't hike into a dead end or have an epic finding a different way off.

Having more than one option is crucial in case of bad routefinding on the way down or bad weather. If your new route is near an established route, check to see whether you can rappel down that one or use the walk-off descent it uses. Be prepared for a retreat in any scenario and have a safe and quick escape plan.

BOLTING

Place a bolt only when absolutely necessary. The basic rule is to place bolts only where you can't get anything else to work. Even then, be sure you really need it because once you place it, there's no turning back.

People argue that bolts shouldn't be used, period. They argue that if you can't do a route without them, then it shouldn't be done. I disagree. If you place the highest priority on very minimal bolting, you can create a high-end route that demands respect. Big walls have blank sections between features that can't be ascended any other way.

Imagine that you'd led to the end of the rope on hooks. You'd *have* to drill an anchor, unless you're crazy enough to belay and haul on hooks! Drilling a bat hook is the same in principle as drilling a bolt. If you drill a hole, you should fill it. In fact, when you bat-hook, you can't high-step and reach as far to drill the next one, forcing you to drill more holes than if you had used rivets.

When putting up a new route, maintain the highest standards and leave the drill at home or in the bag, drilling only when you absolutely have to.

If the area you're climbing in has a strict code of ethics, follow them to the minutest detail. If you can use natural protection, including pitons, use them instead of drilling. Follow and respect the style in which the area was pioneered, and follow all laws, including regulations in national parks.

As climbers, we need to police our actions ourselves. By using poor judgment when it comes to being ethically responsible, we could put our resources in jeopardy for future generations. Be responsible and accountable for your actions.

SOLO CLIMBING

For some climbers, the wall experience is better done solo. I've soloed walls and found the silence and solitude rejuvenating, adding a depth to the experience that I didn't have with a partner. The workload is triple the amount and the mental challenges are greater for a solo climber; however, the rewards are also greater. After you've finished a route solo, you have a greater sense of accomplishment and pride, in addition to believing in yourself.

Climbing solo has its benefits. Not having a partner allows you to be on any schedule you want, to climb fast or slow, to sleep in late, to not have to shout out, to lead every pitch, to take in the experience on a deeper level, to push yourself, and to be in complete control. When soloing, there's no one to answer to or share with; it's just you, the climbing, and your surroundings. Occasionally birds swoop in for a closer look, the winds whisper, and the ringing of hammer on iron echoes over the sound of your own breathing. The solitude of solo climbing fills the void we often overlook—our need to be alone within ourselves—by being consumed with life's daily routines and interactions with others. The inner self has time to open up and be in the present. When you're leading solo, everything other than the connection with the current experience is removed and you enter into a rhythm that's balanced, the outer with the inner. The tasks of wall climbing may be demanding, but they are peripheral in comparison with what's going on inside your head. There's no partner to distract you from your thoughts. Leading, cleaning, and hauling take their toll, but at the end of the day, a relaxing mental and physical state overcomes any anxiety.

Climbing solo also has its drawbacks, the worst of which is the amount of labor involved. Leading, rappelling, cleaning, then hauling each pitch feels as though you're climbing the pitch three times, and this is extra demanding. It can also just take a lot longer to climb solo, which can be a real issue when the weather is unpredictable. Another drawback is how mentally draining solo climbing can be. Keeping your psyche up while controlling any fears or anxiety can leave you more drained than the physical climbing. It is common to feel insecure in the face of soloing a wall, and this can turn you back. In the event of a retreat, not having a partner makes it that much more daunting. You also can't blame anyone but yourself for making mistakes.

One of the great wall soloists, Jim Beyer, has pushed the limits of aid climbing and solo wall climbing. Climbing almost exclusively solo, Jim has climbed first ascents in Pakistan, Baffin Island, the Black Canyon of the Gunnison, Yosemite, and the desert Southwest, to name just a few. His determination to finish Project Mayhem (VII, 5.11, A5) on the 4000-foot west face of Mount Thor on Baffin Island carried over two years of hard work, all solo. His subgrading of aid ratings goes so far as to include how sketchy the belays are, often built of multiple placements strung together to avoid drilling bolts. He has introduced potential A6 routes that encompass an A5 pitch over a bogus anchor that would fail in the event of a fall. His routes seldom see repeats.

Another solo climber, Dean Potter, has taken solo free climbing walls to a new level in the past several years. His many rope-free ascents in Yosemite shattered previous speed records while ushering in a new realm of climbing big walls solo. His solo linkup of Half Dome and El Capitan in a day marked a profound new dimension that he took even further when he soloed Cerro Torre and Fitzroy (twice) in Patagonia, Argentina, in 2002. His experiences on the big cliffs of Yosemite prepared him mentally and physically for the commitment necessary on the alpine peaks in Patagonia.

There are many ways a solo climber can ascend a wall, and the limits are only mental. Russel Mitchrovich climbed El Capitan's Zodiak without a rope, using three daisy chains as his only means of being connected to the wall: his must be one of the wildest ascents ever done on a big wall, with the consequence of making a mistake being final.

To be a solo climber, master all the techniques in this book, including the ones in this chapter. Reading about these techniques won't give you the full set of tools you need to go solo the way hands-on experience will, so go out and practice at a small crag before you commit to a wall. Climb several big walls with a partner before you take on a solo project. The more you have the systems dialed, the more fun you'll have. To embark on a wall solo is liberating and demanding. The challenge makes you define yourself in a way nothing else can.

SELF-BELAY TECHNIQUES

First and foremost in solo belaying is building a multidirectional anchor that can withstand a leader fall that 98 percent of the time is in an upward direction. The leader climbs carrying the entire rope, with one end fixed to the anchor and the other to the harness, allowing slack while climbing to pass through a belay device that will catch in the event of a fall.

Belay methods. For solo climbing, belay methods range from a clove hitch on a locking biner attached to your harness to an autolocking belay device. The clove hitch is the slowest and most manual self-belay technique, but it works if you don't have a solo belay device. Here's how:

1. Attach one end of the lead rope to the anchor and then a clove hitch to a locking biner on your harness's tie-in point, with enough slack between the anchor and the locking biner to make at least one movement at a time.

2. Adjust the amount of slack between the anchor and your harness to make upward progress.

3. If you plan on climbing a section free, use two locking biners attached to your belay loop, each with a clove hitch on it and a length of slack long enough to make it past the free section. Before you start the free section, unclip the loop and free climb past the section or till you reach the next loop.

The self-belay devices automatically slide the rope through, providing a system that requires no manual adjustment as you climb. Wren Industries makes three solo belay devices: the Silent Partner, the Solo-Aid, and the Soloist. Five other self-locking devices include the Petzl GriGri, the Trango Cinch, the SRC from Wild Country, Camp's Yo-Yo, and Alp Tech's ABS. All these devices are suitable for solo climbing when used properly. A GriGri, which isn't designed for use as a solo device, has been used as such for years. The GriGri can be modified to feed automatically. Here's how:

1. Drill a small hole through the metal and plastic at a diagonal on the hinged end on the brake-hand side.

2. Place a piece of wire through the hole and swage it closed (like a small circle head) so it makes a 1-inch circle, just enough to clip a biner through.

3. Clip this in to your chest harness to hold the device vertically, allowing the rope to feed through by itself as you move up. This modified loop doesn't need to support your weight or be full strength; it's just to hold the device upright.

4. Use caution and remember to always tie a backup knot.

If you don't modify the GriGri, it'll still work, but you'll have to manually feed the

A customized GriGri for using as a solo belay device

rope through it; otherwise, it tends to autolock as you're climbing.

Belay anchors. Build a multidirectional belay anchor and use one of the above belay methods to lead each pitch. Because a solo fall creates more force on the anchor, two methods are used to reduce the amount of force created. In the first, you add a screamer (a load-reducing sling) to the anchor, which reduces the amount of force put on the anchor and gear placements during a fall. Here's how:

1. Clip the screamer to the power point, the same place you clipped in the lead rope (see Figure 21).

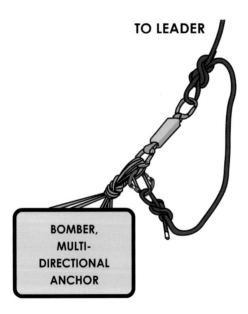

TO LEADER

BOMBER, MULTI-DIRECTIONAL ANCHOR

Figure 21. *Clip a screamer in to the belay to reduce the anchor's potential for shock loading.*

2. Tie a figure eight on a bight 2 feet from the anchored end of the lead rope, and clip the other end of the screamer in here.

3. Now if you take a fall, the screamer will take the force directly. If it fully activates or comes unclipped, the lead rope is still clipped in directly to the anchor.

The second way to reduce the amount of force on the belay anchor is to clip your haul bag in to the power point (see Figure 22) so that if you fall, the haul bag acts as deadweight and is lifted up, absorbing much of the impact force just as a belayer would.

If you're climbing without a haul bag and are mostly free soloing over easier terrain but find a section you want a belay for, you can use a different belay technique. If you find fixed gear such as a bolt on the pitch, put a biner on it, clip the rope in so it's looped from your harness to your device, and continue upward using your autolocking belay device. When you get to a secure place above or stop on a ledge, simply untie and pull the rope through as if pulling a rappel. You'll have to leave the biner behind, but it's faster than having to rappel and jumar back up. This isn't as safe as traditional solo belay techniques, and the piece has to be failsafe.

LEADING SOLO

As with any lead, carry only what you need. Extra weight slows you down, especially when you're soloing. That said, bring a double portaledge for the added

TO LEADER   **HAUL LINE**

Figure 22. *Using the haul bag as a belay shock absorber*

room and comfort, because it's hardly any heavier than a single portaledge.

Stack the haul line in a rope bag or in a way that it'll feed out clean and not get stuck as you climb. When you're finished with the lead, build a multidirectional anchor so it's ready to go for the next lead.

The next step is to fix the lead rope, set up the haul, and get ready to clean the pitch. There are several ways to set this up. Here's the best way:

1. Fix the lead rope to the anchor. Leave the rack, and anything else you don't need for cleaning, at the anchor.
2. Set up the haul line for hauling and pull the haul bag up off the lower anchor by 1–2 feet, leaving it clipped in to that anchor by its daisy chain.
3. Rappel the lead rope, clipping each piece back in to the rope as you pass it.
4. Release the haul bag from the anchor. By hauling the bag a few feet off the lower anchor, all you have to do is unclip its daisy from the anchor. Lower it out if necessary.
5. Set up your jumars on the lead rope and clean the anchor and the pitch.
6. Haul the bag to the anchor and get ready for the next lead.

As an alternative, you can rappel the haul line: this is a better way to return to the lower anchor if the pitch is overhanging or traversing.

Dealing with multiple ropes can be cumbersome. When leading solo, you can tie the lead rope in to bomber pieces along the way to act as intermediate anchors. This takes the weight of the rope below that piece off you and can help prevent the rope from rubbing against sharp edges when you're leading or cleaning. You can stack the lead rope in a rope bag and carry it with you or clip long loops of rope to your harness as backups to the device to manage it better as you lead. If you use long loops,

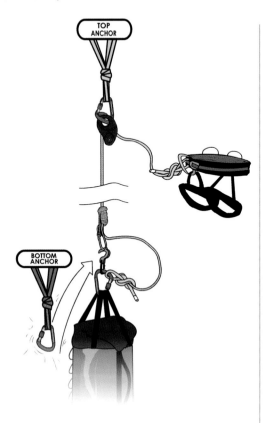

Figure 23. *Closeup of a fifi haul*

be careful to clip the lead rope to each placement, because sometimes you'll have more than one loop hanging off your harness. The fewer loops you have, the more streamlined the system.

HAULING SOLO

To haul solo, you can use a fifi hook and prusik knot. This can be risky because it requires precise setup and the prusik might

not always engage. Here's how it works:

1. Tie the fifi hook to the haul bag; the fifi hook holds the haul bag on the anchor until you're ready to haul (see Figure 23).
2. Clip a prusik knot in to the fifi hook's top hole and tie the prusik to the haul line above the knot on the haul line.
3. When you start to haul, the prusik will clamp onto the haul line and pull the fifi hook off the anchor: this allows you to haul the bag before or after rappelling and cleaning without someone else to release it.

Another way is to rappel to the anchor on the haul line, lift or minihaul the haul bag off the anchor, and lower it out so it hangs on the pulley-haul setup on the upper anchor, then haul it once you've cleaned the pitch.

A final way to haul is tricky; it works only with lighter loads, and you must use special care in setting it up. You need three ropes for it to work: one lead rope, one haul rope, and one rappel rope. Here's how you do it:

1. Fix the lead rope after leading the pitch.
2. Set up the haul rope through the pulley system and clip the end of it to your belay loop (see Figure 24).
3. Fix the third rope for rappelling and set up your rappel.
4. With the haul bag set up on the fifi hook as in the first method described above, you'll counterweight-haul the bag as you rappel to the anchor below.

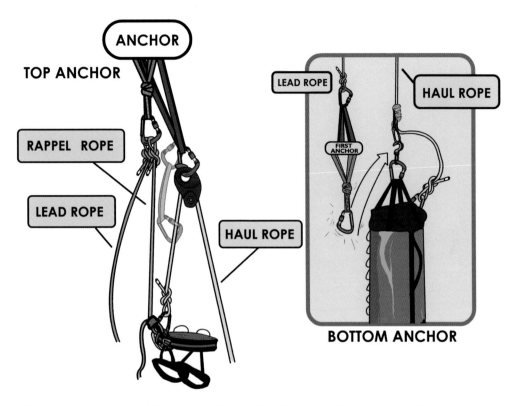

TOP ANCHOR

ANCHOR

RAPPEL ROPE

LEAD ROPE

HAUL ROPE

LEAD ROPE

HAUL ROPE

FIRST ANCHOR

BOTTOM ANCHOR

Figure 24. *Three-rope haul for a solo climber: as the climber rappels on one rope, his or her weight pulls the haul bag off the anchor and up as he or she goes down.*

5. Get off the rappel rope and jumar on the lead line to clean the pitch. . Simple!

The main issue with this setup is that if for some reason the fifi hook were to come off the anchor—say, during a leader fall—the haul bag would fall the full length of the haul line and fall directly onto your harness, a sure disaster. This system needs careful setup. Practice this system and have it dialed if you plan to use it on a long route.

CHAPTER 4

Mark Synnott on the first ascent of Ship of Fools (VII 5.11+ A2 M6), on Shipton Spire, Pakistan

Self-Rescue

Climbing walls is a self-reliant activity, and part of that self-reliance includes self-rescue. If you get into a bad situation, in which you or your partner become injured and need to be rescued, self-rescue is the number-one resource. It is usually the fastest way to get out of a bad situation and should always be implemented unless you absolutely have to call for a rescue.

Calling in a rescue puts you and your rescuers in more danger than if you were able to implement a self-rescue. By being knowledgeable about self-rescue techniques and preparing properly to be self-contained on any wall adventure, you're more likely to be able to sit through a storm or retreat with a victim safely and quickly.

PREPARATION

This chapter covers the basic skills necessary to facilitate a self-rescue. However, there are complete books on rescue that are more in-depth and thorough, and you should read these. This chapter is only a brief summary of the tools and steps involved in performing a self-rescue. These methods are complex and require practice to perform properly. Refer to a self-rescue book for complete instruction.

There are several ways an accident could happen on a wall. Most injuries happen when a climber has fallen or been hit by a falling object. In any situation, the uninjured climber will have to perform the rescue tasks, whether that climber is leading or belaying at the time. Later in this chapter are some scenarios in which a climber needs to be rescued and the steps to take to perform these rescues.

TOOLS FOR SELF-RESCUE

Fortunately, as wall climbers we carry excellent tools to facilitate a self-rescue. You'll obviously have a harness, and you might also have a chest harness (helpful for rescuing an unconscious victim). You'll also have plenty of slings and biners. These all make organizing and managing a rescue faster and safer. In addition to these, here are the basic tools you need:

- Two cordelettes
- Accessory cord for prusiks (shoulder-length runners can work too)
- Oval or D carabiners (work best)
- Locking carabiners
- Belay/rappel device
- Two ropes
- Pair of jumars (work better than prusiks)

KNOTS FOR SELF-RESCUE

These knots allow you to perform tasks specific to rescue, and all climbers going up a big wall should know them. Keep in mind that Spectra material isn't suited well for friction knot situations because it is weaker when heated.

- Figure eight (figure eight follow-through and figure eight on a bight): for tying in to the rope
- Prusik knot, Klemheist knot, autoblock, Bachmann knot: friction knots
- Mariner knot, mule knot, Münter-mule knot combination: load transfer knots
- Münter hitch: belay/rappel knot

KEY EXERCISE: TYING RESCUE KNOTS

Practice making and using each of these knots: figure eight, prusik, Klemheist, autoblock, Bachmann, mariner, mule, Münter, and Münter-mule combination. Try using both accessory cord and webbing to see how they work. Practice until you can make and use them efficiently.

THE SIX STEPS IN ACCIDENT RESPONSE

In any rescue situation, follow these six steps:

1. Survey the scene to prevent any further problems or injuries.
2. Determine any first-aid needs, if necessary.
3. Create a plan of action.
4. Build your rescue system.
5. Recheck your system.
6. Begin the rescue.

RESCUING THE LEADER

STEP 1

Escape the belay and ascend to the victim.

1. Lower the victim either back to you or to the closest reliable anchor point. Be sure you can place more protection at the place to where you lower the victim, because you'll be rappelling with or lowering the victim from this point.
2. Escape the belay by first using a mule knot to lock off the belay device to free both your hands, then place a prusik knot on the loaded rope above your belay and tie a Münter-mule knot or a mariner knot to the anchor in an upward pulling position. Back it up with a figure eight clipped in to the anchor with 3 feet of slack. Reinforce your anchor for an upward pull and then remove yourself from the belay system.
3. Ascend to the victim on the loaded lead rope using jumars or prusiks

(you won't be able to tie backup knots).

STEP 2

Build an anchor, attach the victim, descend to the previous anchor to free the rope, then ascend and clean the pitch back to the victim.

1. Build a reinforced anchor point (bring gear or use the gear on the leader's rack) at the place to which you lowered the victim, and attach the victim to it (with a girth-hitched sling from the leader's harness) using a Münter-mule or mariner knot, in addition to another girth-hitched sling and a locking biner as backup (this needs to be slack): the weight must be on the mariner or Münter-mule so you can release the victim off the anchor when lowering. Make the anchor below the point of protection the victim was lowered on, because this upper point of protection is what you will use as a directional to lower the victim with.
2. Attach the rope to the new anchor using a prusik so you weight the anchor as you descend and reascend the rope.
3. Descend to the previous anchor by down-jumarring.
4. Disassemble the previous anchor by first removing the backup figure eight knot. Then unload the anchor by releasing the mariner and/or Münter-mule knot to free the rope. Clean the remaining anchor unless you plan to

use it as the next rappel anchor. Now you can jumar and clean the pitch up to the victim. The rope is fixed to the new anchor with the prusik and is backed up by the victim's weight through the pieces of protection above him or her. Clip in to the anchor point.

STEP 3

Lower the victim with the rope (tie a knot in the end for safety) by putting him or her on belay and tying a mule knot. Remove the backup and mariner knots so the victim lowers onto your belay device that's backed up by the mule knot, then untie the mule knot and proceed to lower the victim to the next rappel anchor or the ground. Once you have the victim on the ground, seek out a ground rescue and get the victim to a hospital.

COUNTERWEIGHT OR ASSISTED RAPPEL

If the victim needs assistance, do a counterweight rappel or assisted rappel. To perform a counterweight rappel using a single rope:

1. Tie the victim in to one end and lower on the other end of the rope as you rappel it (tie a knot in the end of the rope or, better yet, tie in to the end of the rope yourself). Use an autoblock knot tied below the belay device for safety.
2. Once you reach the next anchor, lock off the rappel with the autoblock, tie a backup knot on the rappel ropes,

attach the victim to the anchor using a Münter-mule or mariner knot and a backup sling with a locking biner, attach yourself to the anchor, and lower both of you onto the new anchor.
3. Now untie from the end of the rope, retrieve the rope, and set up the next rappel as you did the last one until you reach the ground.

If you have two ropes in this scenario, you will have to pass a knot on the way down (see Passing Knots in Chapter 2, Basic Wall-Climbing Procedures) and untie the victim to retrieve the ropes.

To perform an assisted rappel:

1. Attach a rappel device and a locking biner to the ropes.
2. Attach both the victim and yourself to the same locking biner at equal or offset lengths so you can see where you're going. Use an autoblock knot on the rappel for safety.
3. Remove both of the climber's backups from the anchor and rappel to the next anchor.
4. Continue assisted rappelling until you reach the ground.

ASSISTING THE LEADER TO LOWER

If the leader has to be lowered back to the anchor, but there isn't enough rope to make it back:

1. Lower the leader to the lowest reliable anchor point and reinforce it to make an anchor.
2. Have the leader clip in to the anchor

point with a girth-hitched sling and locking biner, then tie a figure eight on a bight from your end of the rope to the leader's harness through the new anchor, with two opposite and opposed biners or a locking biner.

3. Have the leader untie from the end of the rope while still on belay, retrieve the rope from above, tie back in to the end of the rope, untie the figure eight, and allow you to pull in the slack.

4. Take in the slack and the leader's weight, remove the backup to the anchor, and lower the leader back to your anchor.

RESCUING THE SECOND

WITH TWO ROPES

This method is used when you are belaying the second climber up and the rope is not fixed for the second to jumar on.

1. Lower the second back to the previous anchor or down to a reliable anchor point and reinforce it. The second clips in to the new anchor using a locking biner and a sling, if able to assist. If the second can't assist, clip him or her in to the new anchor with a Münter-mule or mariner knot and a backup once you get to the second.

2. Once the second has been lowered into position, escape the belay using a prusik with a mariner or Münter-mule knot to the anchor backed up

with a figure eight that's also clipped to the anchor, and set up a counterweight rappel using the lead rope and the second rope tied together.

3. Remove the backup figure eight from the anchor, set up your rappel device, and tie a mule knot to lock it off. Release the mariner or Münter-mule knot that was holding the victim to weight your device, and remove the mule knot that locked it off. Rappel to the victim using a counterweight rappel. Provide first aid if necessary.

4. Clip the victim in to the new anchor with a Münter-mule or mariner knot and a backup, unless he or she already clipped in to the anchor and is able to assist.

5. Clip yourself in to the anchor, untie from the ropes, retrieve the ropes, and set up another rappel.

6. Repeat lowering, assisted rappelling, or counterweight rappelling until you reach the ground.

WITH ONE ROPE

This method is used if you are belaying the second up.

1. Lock off the belay with a mule knot, use a prusik and a Münter-mule or mariner knot to secure the victim's rope to the anchor and a backup figure eight to the anchor, and escape the belay. Fix the rest of the lead rope to the anchor with a figure eight on a bight: you'll use this to rappel.

2. Descend to the victim on the remainder of rope if there is enough length

to get to him or her. If not, use prusiks (or jumars) to descend to the victim on the loaded lead rope and administer first aid if necessary.

3. Build a new anchor and attach the victim to it, using a Münter-mule or mariner knot backed up with another sling to the anchor.

4. Ascend to the upper anchor and lower the victim onto the new anchor by putting him or her back on belay with a mule knot to lock off the device, removing the Münter-mule or mariner knot and the backup figure eight, and lowering the victim onto the new anchor.

5. Set up a counterweight rappel and descend to the victim.

6. Retrieve the rope and continue the descent using counterweight or assisted rappels.

ON A FIXED ROPE

1. Fix a second rope to your anchor and use it to rappel to the victim, or down-jumar or prusik the fixed rope the second is on to get to him or her.

2. Build an anchor and attach the victim to it using a Münter-mule or mariner knot and another sling with a locking biner as a backup.

3. Have the victim release his or her jumars or prusiks off the rope to transfer his or her weight onto the new anchor.

4. Ascend to the upper anchor, unfix the rope the victim was on, and set up a rappel.

5. Descend to the victim and clip in to the anchor. Pull the ropes and continue the descent using counterweight or assisted rappels or lowering.

If the victim cannot assist you in releasing his or her jumars or prusiks off the fixed rope and onto the new anchor:

1. Tie the victim in to the end of the second rope, ascend to the upper anchor, and, using a 3:1 hauling system (see Chapter 2, Basic Wall-Climbing Procedures), hoist the victim up 1–2 feet until he or she unweights the fixed line.

2. Set up a prusik on the haul line below the 3:1 and attach it to the anchor using a Münter-mule or mariner knot backed up to the anchor with a figure eight. Lower the victim onto the prusik and remove the 3:1 system.

3. Continue with one of the methods described above to lower, assisted rappel, or counterweight rappel the victim to the ground.

RAISING WITH A Z-PULLEY SYSTEM

In certain situations, it is better to raise the victim than to lower him or her. For instance, if you're only a few pitches from the top of a big wall, it's easier to raise the victim to the top rather than lower him or her all the way to the bottom. If there's a clearing or a trail at the top, a rescue party can land a helicopter or hike in to assist with a rescue. However, this is more time consuming and much more difficult to perform, and it requires expert instruction on how to do it safely. If this is the only way out of your situation, set up a Z-pulley (3:1) system (see Figure 14 in Chapter 2, Basic Wall-Climbing Procedures) or a similar hauling system. Read a book on rescue to get thorough instruction, because it's beyond the scope of this book.

FIRST AID

Part of self-rescue on a wall includes being prepared for any medical emergencies, from a bee sting or minor cuts to major medical problems such as broken bones. Being able to recognize when a problem needs more than a bandage is essential to survival, especially when getting to a hospital can take hours, if not days, in the event of a full-blown rescue. There are ways to improvise with what you have on the wall, but a serious injury can turn fatal if you're not prepared.

If you don't know cardiopulmonary resuscitation (CPR), take a class; it's quick and affordable and could save your partner's life. You can take it almost anywhere. Read a wilderness first-aid book or take a class to educate yourself on ways you can treat most illnesses or injuries in the field.

Wall climbing involves suffering in one form or another, but it's better to suffer through just the hard work instead of an injury. Remember, the most important self-rescue skill is to prevent the need for a rescue. Be prepared, climb smart, and be safe.

Glossary

aider: A four- or five-step ladder made of nylon webbing used to make upward progress while aid climbing. *See etrier.*

all-free: A term used when a climb has been done without any use of aid climbing practices to ascend.

alpine style: A method of wall climbing that doesn't involve fixing ropes.

angle: Piton made from bent steel to fit cracks $1/2$–$1^1/2$ inches wide.

ascender: Mechanical clamp that cams onto the rope and slides up but not down. They can be reversed on the rope for downward movement. *See Jumar.*

autoblock knot: A friction hitch used to back up your brake hand when rappelling.

autolocking belay device: A belay device, used for belaying a second climber, that locks the rope automatically in a fall.

back-clean: To remove a previously placed piece of gear while climbing.

beak seam: A micro crack in the rock that accepts only tiny pitons such as birdbeaks for protection. It isn't advised to make a belay off of these micropitons; use bolts for an anchor, instead.

Big Bro: A telescoping tubular piece of protection that uses a camming/wedging action; it can be placed with one hand.

bight: Any bend in the rope that doesn't cross itself; used for creating knots and to thread the rope into belay/rappel devices.

birdbeak: A hooklike micropiton. Also called a beak.

bivy: From bivouac; a marginal place to sleep overnight. Also, to sleep overnight in such a place.

blade: A short term for a knifeblade.

brass wire: A clean aid tool, e.g., a micronut.

Bugaboo: A thick knifeblade piton.

cam: A common term for a spring-loaded camming device, a clean aid tool; hybrid cams have two different sizes of cams on the same unit, perfect for flares or pin scars. Also, to exert a downward force into crack walls as an outward force, creating friction to oppose the downward pull, as when using a cam hook.

cam hook: A simple metal hook that cams against the sides of a crack under body weight.

chockstone: A naturally wedged stone in a crack that may or may not be solid enough to use as an anchor.

circlehead: A copper or aluminum swage on a loop of cable used in horizontal placements.

clean, or clean aid: A description of a route that is free of the need to place pitons.

cleaner biner: A carabiner that is used to clip to pitons prior to cleaning them.

cleaning: Removing protection anchors from a climb.

clove hitch: A knot used for tying a rope in to an anchor or connecting gear to the rope; often used by the climber to clip in to the belay anchors because it's easy to adjust the tie-in length.

coil: A bend in rope or webbing that crosses over itself.

combo device: A mechanical device that has both a pulley and a rope clamp used for hauling and rescue applications.

copper head: A cylindrical copper or aluminum swage on a cable used for incipient grooves when aid climbing.

cordelette: A 16- to 25-foot length of cord usually made from 5 mm to 7 mm cord that's tied into a loop and used to equalize anchors or for rescue.

crux: The most difficult section of a climb or pitch.

daisy chain: A length of webbing or cord with clip-in loops along its entire length, used to connect the climber to a placement, rope, or anchor point.

equalize: To tie the anchor points together so they share any load equally.

etrier: A nylon-webbing ladder used for aid climbing. *See aider*.

expanding: The movement or flexing of a block, crack, or flake under the load of aid placements.

fifi hook: A flat, open hook fastened to a harness, used for resting on placements.

fixed protection: Any permanent anchor point, usually a bolt, piton, or permanently set chock or cam.

French-free: To rest on gear while climbing without aiders.

funkness device: A short length of cable with loops on each end, used for cleaning.

garda hitch: A hauling method useful on long free climbs; also called an alpine clutch.

girth hitch: A knot used to connect a sling or loop of cord to an object by wrapping it around the object and through itself.

GriGri: An autolocking belay device made by Petzl.

haul: The work of getting the gear up a climb.

haul bag: A bag used to hold equipment dragged up a climb.

haul line: A rope used to haul the haul bag.

hex: A short term for hexcentric, a lightweight alternative to a camming device, ideal because a hex doesn't "walk" like a cam and can fit into shallower pockets.

high-stepping: Stepping in the top step of the aider.

hook: A steel hook-shaped device that is set on edges and knobs, available in several shapes and sizes.

jug: Another name for Jumar. *See Jumar.*

jugging: Ascending a fixed rope using jumars.

Jumar: A type of ascender; lowercase, it refers to any generic type of ascender. Also, to ascend a fixed rope.

knifeblade: A thin blade-type piton.

lead: To be first on a climb, placing gear with which to protect oneself.

leapfrog: To remove the previous piece of protection and place it again above.

Leeper cam hook: A small hook available in flat and pointed styles for aid climbing.

Leeper piton: A piton with a Z-shaped cross section.

Lost Arrow: A forged steel piton; also called an LA.

lower out: To lower a climber or haul bag on a rope.

lower-out line: A length of rope used to lower out the haul bags on a traversing pitch.

mechanical advantage: The ratio of load to pull required to lift the load. For example, if 1 kN (kilonewton) of force is required to raise 2 kN, the mechanical advantage is said to be 2:1. Mechanical advantage is gained at the expense of endurance; even though less force is required, it's required over a longer distance.

micropiton: A very short, thin piece of metal; includes birdbeaks, peckers, and RURPs.

Mini Traxion: A small mechanical device with a pulley and rope clamp used for hauling and rescue applications.

mule knot: A knot that ties the rope off onto a belay device; it can be released under load, so it is used in many self-rescue applications.

multidirectional anchor: An anchor that can hold a load in any direction.

Münter hitch: A hitch that creates friction on the rope, used for belaying and rappelling.

Münter-mule: A combination of the Münter hitch and mule knot to create a tie-off that can be released while under load, used in rescue.

nut: A wedge-shaped anchor that locks into a constriction in a crack to create an anchor point.

nut tool: A thin metal pick used to help loosen and remove stuck protection or to clean cracks.

opposition: Points of protection used to oppose each other to create a stronger anchor; without opposition, the individual protection pieces would be poor; sometimes used to create multidirectional anchors.

overhang: A section of rock that is steeper than vertical.

pecker: A micropiton.

pendulum: To swing across a rock face suspended by a rope.

pin: Another word for a piton.

pitch: The section of a climb between two belays.

piton: A steel spike that is hammered into a crack to create an anchor; an eye on the piton provides an attachment point. Also called a pin.

portaledge: A hanging platform on which to sleep.

power point: The main clip-in point on an equalized anchor.

prusik: A friction hitch used in self-rescue systems that creates the highest friction among the friction knots.

quickclip: A girth-hitched loop of webbing attached to the belay loop; used to clip in to anchor points while leading.

quickdraw: A short sling with a carabiner clipped in to each end; used for connecting the rope to bolts, nuts, or other pieces of protection or for extending the protection on an anchor to minimize bending of the rope.

rack: The collection of protection anchors, slings, quickdraws, etc., that the climber uses to climb a pitch.

redirect: To change the direction of pull on a rope by rerouting it through an anchor; often used to run the climber's rope up to a high anchor and back to the belayer, thereby decreasing the load on the belayer and pulling the belayer up rather than down.

RF-welded seam: Radio frequency technology that fuses the material together for a sealed seam.

rope drag: Friction created by the rope running through carabiners and over rock; increases with each bend in the rope.

RP: A micronut.

runout: A relatively long section on a climb where there is no available protection.

RURP: Realized ultimate reality piton, a micropiton created by Yvon Chouinard.

screamer: A load-reducing, tack-stitched sling.

second: The climber who follows the leader up a pitch, cleaning the protection while climbing.

slider nut: A clean aid tool that fits into cracks by a sliding mechanism.

stacking the rope: Flaking out the rope with the top and bottom ends exposed to avoid tangles.

stopper: Another term for nut.

tag line: A rope trailed by the leader for hauling and rappelling. Also called a haul line or a zip line.

tension-traverse: To climb sideways with the aid of a rope held taut between the leader and belayer.

tie-off: Short loop of thin webbing hitched over pitons to change the tie-in point to reduce leverage.

topo: A map of a route using symbols to show the route's features, ratings, and belays.

transition: To change from one system to another; e.g., from following to leading or from leading to rappelling.

traverse: A section of a climb that moves sideways instead of upward.

Tri-cam: A nut-type piece of protection that can be used in three ways.

waste case: A tube used for storing human waste on a climb.

Appendix A. Climbing Resources

CLIMBING ORGANIZATIONS

Access Fund, P.O. Box 17010, Boulder, CO 80308; (303) 545-6772; *www.accessfund.org.*

American Alpine Club, 710 10th Street, Suite 100, Golden, CO 80401; (303) 384-0110; *www.americanalpineclub.org.*

American Mountain Guides Association, P.O. Box 1739, Boulder, CO 80302; (303) 271-0984; *www.amga.com.*

American Safe Climbing Association, P.O. Box 1814, Bishop, CA 93515; (650) 843-1473; *www.safeclimbing.org.*

Leave No Trace, P.O. Box 997, Boulder, CO 80306; (303) 442-8222; *www.lnt.org.*

The Mountaineers Club, 300 Third Avenue West, Seattle, WA 98119; (206) 284-6310; *www.mountaineers.org.*

CLIMBING WEBSITES

www.alpinist.com
www.climberonline.com
www.climbing.com
www.climbingboulder.com
www.climbing-gyms.com
www.climbingjtree.com
www.climbingmoab.com
www.naclassics.com
www.neclimbs.com
www.primenet.com
www.rockandice.com
www.rockandroad.com
www.rockclimbing.com
www.rocklist.com
www.speedclimb.com
www.supertopo.com
www.touchstoneclimbing.com
www.yosemite.com

Appendix B. Walls of the World

Wall climbing has found its way to some of the most remote corners of the globe. This appendix gives you an idea of some of the major wall climbing destinations of the world.

If you travel to any destination that's new, be respectful of local climbing ethics and sensitive to the environment. Traveling on a long expedition is exciting but can also be frustrating and difficult. Dragging all your climbing gear around the globe to climb walls magnifies the intensity of travel in remote areas, but once you get to the climbing, everything falls into place. Wherever you plan to climb, have fun doing it.

NORTH AMERICA

YOSEMITE NATIONAL PARK

Without a doubt, California's Yosemite Valley is the primary destination for wall climbers around the world. The variety of climbing offers every type of terrain, from slabs to overhangs, from boulder problems to 3000-foot walls. From the beginning, Yosemite has defined wall climbing standards, and it remains the premier testing ground for climbers of all levels. Nowhere else on the planet are there such majestic granite walls with quick access, superb rock, a range of route difficulty, and fair weather. Visiting Yosemite is best during the spring and autumn when the days are longer and the consistently cooler temperatures make for excellent climbing.

Whether you want to climb your first wall or your hundredth, Yosemite has hundreds of routes to choose from. Washington Column, a 1500-foot cliff near the eastern end of the valley that is a great introduction to wall climbing, offers classic routes including the Prow, Astroman, and the South Face. The Leaning Tower and Sentinel Rock are two other 1200- to 1400-foot cliffs that offer excellent routes of all levels. Yosemite Falls Wall, the Ribbon Falls area, and smaller cliffs such as Glacier Point Apron and the Cathedral Rocks all offer aid and free climbing as well.

The three main walls in Yosemite that draw climbers are El Capitan, Half Dome, and Mount Watkins. Because Mount Watkins requires a longer approach with fewer route choices, it doesn't see as much traffic, but it offers a more remote setting away from the noise and crowds and feels more like a wilderness experience. Half Dome has a number of excellent routes, including the popular Regular Northwest Face, a great introductory wall with excellent bivy sites and fun climbing. Half Dome is often cooler up high when it's too hot in the valley. El Capitan is probably the most recognized big wall on the planet. Tourists crane their necks to watch climbers making their way up this massive monolith. There's a route for everyone on El Cap: from the East Buttress to the Nose, you can find every grade of difficulty on this wall.

In the surrounding mountains of Yosemite and the Sierra Nevada there are plenty of other climbing objectives, including walls up to 2000 feet high. The approaches keep most climbers away because carrying in all the wall gear takes time and kills motivation.

ZION NATIONAL PARK

Zion National Park in Utah has breathtaking walls and scenery with generally short approaches and excellent climbing objectives. The sandstone cliffs ranging from 600 to 2200 feet tall look, feel, and climb unlike any other rock in the United States. They take some getting used to. The softness of the rock makes repeated hammering of pitons excessively damaging, and today most climbers strive for clean climbing practices here. Classic routes such as Space Shot, Touchstone Wall, Prodigal Sun, Moonlight Buttress, and Monkeyfinger offer excellent free and aid climbing challenges, with most routes requiring two to three days. Spring and autumn are the best times to climb in Zion because it's really hot in the summer.

BLACK CANYON OF THE GUNNISON NATIONAL MONUMENT

Colorado's Black Canyon of the Gunnison is a wild and inspiring place to climb. Its influence on alpinism and adventure free climbing is greater or equal to Yosemite's. The cliffs reach up to 2700 feet tall, rising dramatically out of the narrow canyon above the thunderous Gunnison River. Most of the walls require a long, difficult approach down a gully choked with poison ivy, and once you're down there, the high-standard climbing needs complete commitment. If you decide to bail, you have to rappel and hike back up out of the canyon. The nature of the climbing requires boldness, excellent routefinding, and sharp skills. Spring and autumn are the best times to climb in the Black Canyon.

ROCKY MOUNTAIN NATIONAL PARK

Longs Peak in Colorado's Rocky Mountain National Park is one of the best high-altitude wall climbing venues in North America. Despite a relatively shorter season due to weather, as well as a moderate approach, climbers are lured in to the excellent granite routes soaring up to the summit at more than 14,000 feet. This wall has more free climbs than aid climbs, but it still has an excellent array of objectives to choose from. Most climbers need at least two to three days to hike in and complete a climb.

RED ROCKS

Red Rocks near Las Vegas, Nevada, offers excellent climbing on sandstone cliffs up to 2000 feet tall. Black Velvet and Juniper Canyons offer the highest concentration of climbs, with the Rainbow Wall having mostly aid climbs. As in Zion National Park, the softness of the rock here makes repeated hammering of pitons excessively damaging. The best time to climb in Red Rocks is from September through May.

WIND RIVER RANGE

The Wind River Range in Wyoming is perfect for a wilderness experience on a wall. Mount Hooker is the premier wall, with several routes up to 1600 feet tall on good-quality granite. The 20-mile approach can be done by hiring horses or on foot. There's a short window in the summer to climb here because the approach is more difficult with snow.

EASTERN UNITED STATES

Whitesides Mountain in North Carolina is only 700 feet tall, but it has several aid routes that will keep you on your toes. Cannon Cliff is New Hampshire's proudest wall, and at 1000 feet tall, it is the biggest chunk of stone in the Northeast. There are several quality aid lines and classic free climbs on this cliff.

ALASKA

In the Alaska Range there are almost too many walls to name in this book. The cliffs in the Ruth Gorge and Little Switzerland offer amazing potential, along with established routes on alpine wall terrain. The Kichatna Spires and surrounding peaks are some of the most hostile on the planet, but when the weather is good they are some of the most sought after walls anywhere. In southeast Alaska there's the Devils Thumb, the Mendenhall Towers, and Cathedral Spire among many other relatively unknown walls that have established routes on them but are relatively unexplored and seldom visited.

MEXICO

El Gran Trono Blanco (1700 feet) in the Sierra Juarez Mountains of Baja, Mexico, and El Gigante (3200 feet) in Candameña Canyon in Chihuahua, Mexico, provide wall climbing in remote settings. They offer great road-trip destinations in warmer climates, perfect for a winter climb. There are a few routes to choose from on El Gran Trono Blanco and a few in the El Gigante area. Fall, winter, and spring are good for climbing here.

CANADA

In the Northwest Territories of Canada is the Cirque of the Unclimbables, a stack of classic granite towers featuring excellent free and aid climbing objectives. The main towers include Lotus Flower Tower and Mount Proboscis. Approach is usually by floatplane. June through September is the best time to visit.

The Bugaboos in British Columbia are host to classic towers such as North and South Houser Towers, Snowpatch Spire, and Bugaboo Spire. There are many classic aid and free routes to choose from. Late summer is the best time to climb here.

Not far away is Squamish, featuring walls such as the Chief, an 1800-foot shield of flawless granite. There are lots of aid and free climbs to choose from and it's considered the Yosemite of Canada. Spring through autumn is the best time for climbing here.

Baffin Island, in the northeastern part of Canada, most likely has more granite walls than anywhere on earth. The Sam Ford fjord on the east coast and Auyuittuq National Park in the south have seen climbers scale some of the longest and coldest walls imaginable. Routes are generally very demanding within the cold and harsh environment; the climbing is hard, with the added element of extreme remoteness. Seldom do routes get repeated here. Most wall climbing activity involves first ascents; however, there are plenty of routes to choose from. Finding information about established routes here is difficult. Check back issues of climbing publications and journals. Most parties climb in the summer months when there are plenty of hours of sunlight and manageable temperatures.

GREENLAND

Greenland is an excellent destination for granite wall climbing. The Tasermiut Fjord, in the southern tip of Greenland near the town of Nanortalik, is home to the well-known Ulamertorssuaq massif and the Nalumasortoq pillars. There are many routes established and room for more. Summer is the best time to climb here.

SOUTH AMERICA

THE ANDES

The greatest concentration of wall climbing opportunities in South America lies in Argentina and Chile in the Patagonia region. The Fitzroy area in Argentina and Paine National Park in Chile offer some of the best alpine wall climbing in the world, with lots of established routes and unlimited potential. The place is notorious for horrendous weather; people have waited for months on end to get a single day of clear skies for climbing. The most popular time to climb in this area is from November to March.

In the Peruvian Andes, La Esfinge (17,470 feet) rises up out of the Altiplano, surrounded by giant 19,000-foot peaks. This granite wall has several hard free and aid routes reaching a height just over 17,000 feet. Most parties need at least a month to complete a climb. There are several other wall climbing objectives in the range; however, they are even more alpine than this one. Climb in May through September here.

RAIN-FOREST *TEPUIS*

Venezuela and Guyana have unique formations called *tepuis,* consisting of ryolite and sandstone cliffs rising out of the rain forests for 3000 feet. These *tepuis* are usually very difficult to approach, see nearly endless rainfall, and are infested with scorpions, snakes, and lots of crazy bugs. The potential for free and aid climbs is enormous because there are a few hundred of them, with only a handful of established climbs to date. November through May is the best time to climb here.

EUROPE

The expanse of countries in Europe is too vast to showcase all the wall climbing potential in this book; for instance, the Troll Wall, a 3000-foot face in Norway, has a variety of routes, including the Shield. However, below are the more popular destinations.

THE ALPS

The Alps are stacked with rock, from long limestone cliffs in Switzerland and Austria to the alpine granite of Chamonix, France. Most aid climbing walls are found in Chamonix; the American Direttissima on the Petit Dru in Chamonix is a classic alpine wall well worth the effort. There are also a lot of aid climbs on the Eiger and other classic alpine faces in the Alps. The Original route and the Harlin Direttissima on the north face of the Eiger are such classics. Spring through fall is the best time to climb here.

THE DOLOMITES

In Italy, the Dolomites offer some excellent walls, including the classics in the Tre Cime di Lavaredo group. These towers of various lengths and difficulties give enough diversity for any climber to have a challenging adventure. The Swiss-Italian route (1600 feet) on the north face of the Cima Ouest or the Brandler-Hasse on the north face of Cima Grande are not to be missed. There are thousands of routes to climb in the Dolomites. Summer is the most popular time to climb here.

RUSSIA

The Ak Su valley, in the Ak-Su range of Kyrgazstan's Pamir Alai mountains, contains some of the world's finest alpine granite. This area has been visited heavily over the years by both Russian and international climbers. The peaks reach upward of 16,000 feet high, with climbs up to 4200 feet long. This area is difficult to get to and has been considered hostile in the past few years. Traveling here may be dangerous (there have been kidnappings here, and many militia rebels have been fighting in the area in the past several years), and the climbing certainly is very difficult. June through August have seen the most successful climbing expeditions in the Ak-Su.

ASIA

PAKISTAN

Pakistan has the best granite towers and walls anywhere. Between the Trango Towers area and the Charakusa Valley, in Northern Pakistan, there are hundreds of climbed and unclimbed walls with enough potential to last for many generations to come. Most of the climbing objectives are under 19,000 feet and range in length from a few hundred feet to more than 5000 feet. Traveling to Pakistan is involved, and most climbers often spend two months climbing. Visit during the summer.

INDIA

India is also an amazing area for alpine wall climbing. The northern areas, including the Garhwal, Himachal Pradesh, and Ladakh, are (among others) incredible. The area is stacked with objectives, including the classic peaks of Shivling, Bhagirathi, Thalay Sagar, Changabang, and many others. Most

parties spend two or more months climbing. Summer is the most popular time to climb here.

AFRICA

In Andringitra National Park in Madagascar, there are excellent compact granite towers reaching up to 2600 feet in length. There are several established free and aid routes, with great potential for more. There has been an emphasis on free climbing these walls because they are well featured; however, there are some hard aid routes too. Summer months seem to be when most climbing activity takes place.

Mali, Kenya, and Cameroon also boast excellent wall venues with several climbs done in the past several years.

ANTARCTICA

In the remote part of Queen Maud Land, amazing granite towers jut out of the icecap like razor-sharp teeth. This desolate continent is extremely difficult and very expensive to get to. If you can get here, you're going to have one of the best adventures of your life. October through February is best.

Suggested Reading

Cox, Steven M. and Kris Fulsaas, eds. *Mountaineering: The Freedom of the Hills*, 7th edition. Seattle: The Mountaineers, 2003.

Fasulo, David J. *How to Climb: Self-Rescue.* Evergreen, CO: Chockstone Press, 1997.

Long, John. *Climbing Anchors.* Evergreen, CO: Chockstone Press, 1993.

Long, John and John Middendorf. *Big Walls.* Evergreen, CO: Chockstone Press, 1996.

Luebben, Craig. *Rock Climbing: Mastering Basic Skills.* Seattle: The Mountaineers, 2004.

Scott, Doug. *Big Wall Climbing.* Oxford: Oxford University Press, 1974, 1978.

Soles, Clyde. *Climbing: Training for Peak Performance.* Seattle: The Mountaineers, 2002.

——*Expedition Planning.* Seattle: The Mountaineers, 2003.

Wilkerson, James A. *Medicine for Mountaineering*, 5th edition. Seattle: The Mountaineers, 2001.

Index

About the Author

Jared Ogden is a professional climber, photographer, and freelance writer living in Durango, Colorado, with his wife, Kristin, and son, Tobin. His fascination with big wall climbing began at the age of 20 while attending Fort Lewis College in Durango, and since then it has led him to remote corners of the globe in search of first ascents on some of the biggest walls ever climbed. A well rounded climber, he has mastered his style of climbing, from aiding up the alpine walls of the Trango Towers in Pakistan to free climbing the hardest routes in Colorado's Black Canyon of the Gunnison.

Off the walls, Ogden has written articles and sold photographs to such publications as *National Geographic, Men's Journal, Men's Health, Shape Magazine, Climbing, Rock & Ice, Trail Runner, Alpinist, Sports Illustrated for Women, Outside,* and *Outdoor Retailer.*

Photo by Averill Ogden

THE MOUNTAINEERS, founded in 1906, is a nonprofit outdoor activity and conservation club whose mission is "to explore, study, preserve, and enjoy the natural beauty of the outdoors. . . . " Based in Seattle, Washington, the club is now the third-largest such organization in the United States, with 15,000 members and five branches throughout Washington State.

The Mountaineers sponsors both classes and year-round outdoor activities in the Pacific Northwest, which include hiking, mountain climbing, ski-touring, snowshoeing, bicycling, camping, kayaking, nature study, sailing, and adventure travel. The club's conservation division supports environmental causes through educational activities, sponsoring legislation, and presenting informational programs.

All club activities are led by skilled, experienced instructors, who are dedicated to promoting safe and responsible enjoyment and preservation of the outdoors.

If you would like to participate in these organized outdoor activities or the club's programs, consider a membership in The Mountaineers. For information and an application, write or call The Mountaineers, Club Headquarters, 300 Third Avenue West, Seattle, WA 98119; 206-284-6310. You can also visit the club's website at *www.mountaineers.org* or contact The Mountaineers via email at *clubmail@mountaineers.org.*

The Mountaineers Books, an active, nonprofit publishing program of the club, produces guidebooks, instructional texts, historical works, natural history guides, and works on environmental conservation. All books produced by The Mountaineers Books fulfill the club's mission.

Send or call for our catalog of more than 500 outdoor titles:

The Mountaineers Books
1001 SW Klickitat Way, Suite 201
Seattle, WA 98134
800-553-4453
mbooks@mountaineersbooks.org
www.mountaineersbooks.org

The Mountaineers Books is proud to be a corporate sponsor of Leave No Trace, whose mission is to promote and inspire responsible outdoor recreation through education, research, and partnerships. The Leave No Trace program is focused specifically on human-powered (nonmotorized) recreation.

Leave No Trace strives to educate visitors about the nature of their recreational impacts as well as offer techniques to prevent and minimize such impacts. Leave No Trace is best understood as an educational and ethical program, not as a set of rules and regulations.

For more information, visit *www.LNT.org* or call 800-332-4100.

OTHER TITLES IN THE MOUNTAINEERS OUTDOOR EXPERT SERIES

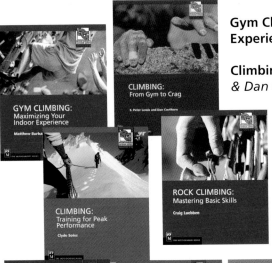

Gym Climbing: Maximizing Your Indoor Experience, *Matt Burbach*

Climbing: From Gym to Crag, *S. Peter Lewis & Dan Cauthorn*

Climbing: Training for Peak Performance, *Clyde Soles*

Rock Climbing: Mastering Basic Skills, *Craig Luebben*

Alpine Climbing: Techniques to Take You Higher, *Mark Houston & Kathy Cosley*

Ice & Mixed Climbing: Modern Technique, *Will Gadd*

Climbing: Expedition Planning, *Clyde Soles & Phil Powers*

OTHER TITLES YOU MIGHT ENJOY FROM THE MOUNTAINEERS BOOKS

Mountaineering: The Freedom of the Hills, *The Mountaineers.*
The climber's bible—complete, authoritative instruction in an easy-to-use format.

The Outdoor Knots Book, *Clyde Soles.* A guide to the ropes and knots used in the outdoors by hikers, campers, paddlers, and climbers. One of the best resources for climbing knots available.

Fifty Favorite Climbs: The Ultimate North American Tick List, *Mark Kroese.*
Fifty elite climbers share their favorite routes—a celebration of contemporary climbing history and the climbers who have shaped it.

Available at fine bookstores and outdoor stores, by phone at 800-553-4453, or on the Web at *www.mountaineersbooks.org*

THE MOUNTAINEERS BOOKS